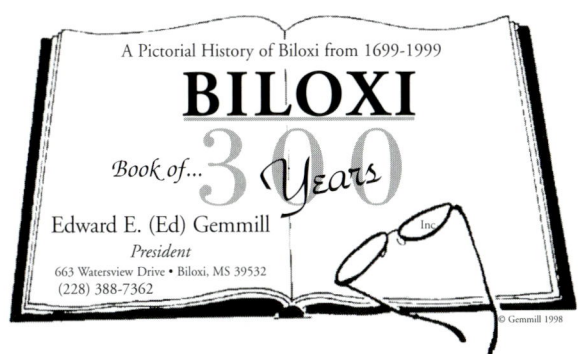

A Pictorial History of Biloxi from 1699-1999

BILOXI

Book of... 300 Years

Edward E. (Ed) Gemmill
President
663 Watersview Drive • Biloxi, MS 39532
(228) 388-7362

As you peruse these pages, you are part of history—a wonderful, colorful, and rich history that we all share and cherish. It's not merely the history of Biloxi, but an important part of the history of the United States of America. In addition to being one of the oldest settlements in the United States, Biloxi also served as the first capital of the Louisiana Territory. This led to the settlement of all of the area between the Mobile River and Mexico, and all of the lands between the Rockies and the Appalachians. Think about it. A huge portion of the United States can trace its beginnings to Biloxi.

In the 1980s, as president of the Biloxi Jaycees, I was involved in the production and marketing of a commemorative book called *Biloxi and the Mississippi Gulf Coast: A Pictorial History.* That book was extremely successful, and I decided that with the dramatic growth we have witnessed since then, and with the Tricentennial approaching in 1999, it was time for an update. The result is *Biloxi: 300 Years.*

I want to thank Mayor A. J. Holloway; Biloxi Public Affairs Manager, Vincent Creel; Attorney, Michael B. McDermott of the firm Page, Mannino, Peresich, Dickinson & McDermott; Attorney, Robert Gambrell; Accountant, DeeDee Patterson Munro and the hundreds of people who have voiced their heartfelt support for this project. Historian Val Husley, Ph.D., has done a tremendous job of accurately tracing the history of our community. Oldtimers will rekindle memories when they look over these pages. Newcomers will discover why Biloxi is such a special place to live and work. For visitors, it's a chance to witness the celebration of our way of life.

Finally, I dedicate this book to my daughter, Kaeley Nicole Gemmill, and the future generations who will make their own history here in Biloxi. By learning about this community's heritage, they will have a stronger appreciation for who we are and where we are going.

Thank you,

Edward E. Gemmill

Edward E. Gemmill
President
Book of Biloxi 300 Years, Inc.

It is truly an honor and a pleasure to have been a part of this project, which has created such a fitting tribute to Biloxi on her 300th anniversary. We are proud of *Biloxi: 300 Years* for providing for posterity the compelling chronicle of our city's first three centuries. We applaud Dr. Val Husley whose painstaking research and uncompromising commitment to accuracy have made this book stand unique among similar endeavors to profile a city's past. This book's thoughtful text and vivid photography bring Biloxi's history to life in an unflinching portrait of a people rich with cultural diversity and blessed with remarkable resilience.

We consider *Biloxi: 300 Years* to be a fair jewel in the crown of Biloxi's Tricentennial celebration, and as co-chairs of the Biloxi Tricentennial Commission, we proudly acknowledge the Commission's role as a major sponsor of this project. It is with solid conviction that we predict this book shall be treasured by many for generations to come.

Sincerely,

Gwen Hand Gollotte & C. Bruce Stewart
Co-Chairs, Biloxi Tricentennial Commission
Board of Directors

BILOXI
WRITTEN BY VAL HUSLEY, Ph.D.

300 Years

Presented by
CITY OF BILOXI

THE DONNING COMPANY PUBLISHERS

To Jacob and Salome Hösli, whose quest for a better life brought them from Glarus, Switzerland, to Biloxi in the 1850s. And to Joe and Coleen Scholtes, whose infectuous love of Biloxi's history and willingness to share were inspirational.

Copyright © 1998 by Dr. Val Husley

All rights reserved, including the right to reproduce this work in any form whatsoever without permission in writing from the publisher, except for brief passages in connection with a review. For information write:

The Donning Company/Publishers
184 Business Park Drive Suite 106
Virginia Beach, VA 23462

Steve Mull, General Manager
Nancy Schneiderheinze, Project Director
Paula Ridge and Ed Schneiderheinze,
    Project Research Coordinators
Dawn V. Kofroth, Assistant General Manager
Sally C. Davis, Associate Editor
Paul C. Gualdoni Jr., Graphic Designer
Teri S. Arnold, Senior Marketing Coordinator

Library of Congress Cataloging-in-Publication Data

Husley, Val, 1941–
        Biloxi : 300 years / written by Val Husley.
            p.   cm.
        Includes bibliographical references and index.
        ISBN 1-57864-039-3
        1. Biloxi (Miss.)—History. 2. Biloxi (Miss.)—History—Pictorial
works.   I. Title.
F349.B5H87 1998
976.2' 13—dc21   98-7936
                                                                CIP

Printed in the United States of America

Contents

Foreword 6

Acknowledgments 7

Introduction 8

Chapter 1: The Earliest Biloxians 10

Chapter 2: Americanization: Birth of a Resort 22

Chapter 3: Birth of a Modern City 38

Chapter 4: Between the Wars 118

Chapter 5: Before Camille and After Camille 140

Chapter 6: Toward a New Millennium 158

Bibliography 168

Index 172

About the Author 176

Foreword

Office of the Mayor

FAX: (228) 435-6129
http://biloxi.ms.us

P.O. Box 429
Biloxi, Mississippi 39533
(228) 435-6254

For three centuries, residents and visitors alike have shared in the unique character that is Biloxi, a city of inimitable charm, soothing tranquility and Southern grace. Its history of hospitality is now enjoying a renaissance that is transforming Biloxi into a major destination resort that promises an even greater future for one of the oldest communities in America.

Inside "Biloxi: 300 Years," you will discover the rich history of this colorful community from its days as a sleepy fishing village, to its reign as the "Seafood Capital of the World," and through the devastation of killer hurricanes like Camille, and the monumental rebuilding effort.

Historian Val Husley brings Biloxi's story to life through his well-crafted words and period photographs. As you turn these pages to discover all the secrets of our city's past, consider the diverse cultural underpinnings that helped shape Biloxi's singular character.

The future of our city is certainly unlimited, but its past is a story worth knowing to anyone who has lived here or visited.

Thank you for being part of history.

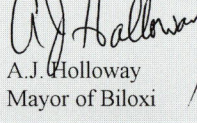

A.J. Holloway
Mayor of Biloxi

Acknowledgments

Books are usually written by one heart but many hands. *Biloxi: 300 Years* was no exception. Many helped by sharing their image collections, digging for materials, and providing guidance and encouragement. Among these, in no particular order of degree of toleration or aggravation are Randy Randazzo, Alan Santa Cruz, Larry Cosper, George Cully, Edmond Boudreaux, Robert Brooks,, Murella Powell, Mimi Stephenson, and the museum gang: Robin, Richard, Marsha, and Lee. For the opportunity to chronicle Biloxi's first three hundred years I must thank the Biloxi Tricentennial Commission and Edward E. Gemmill, President of Book of Biloxi: 300 Years, Inc., whose trust in my historical pursuit made possible this effort. Special thanks, however, are reserved for my wife Shannon, editor-in-chief, critic, and counselor, who got me through yet another "project."

Introduction

For three hundred years Biloxi has enjoyed a hospitable location on the Mississippi Sound and an abundance of seafood. These dual attributes have attracted Native American and European settlement, birthed and nourished an antebellum resort, spurred the development of a canning industry, lured a major military establishment, and provided the foundation for an international tourist destination.

Often accused of being "the best kept secret in the South," Biloxi experienced a slower rate of growth than many other maritime communities. The cosmopolitan composition of its citizenry, whose ethnic diversity evoked a certain *joie de vivre*, however, lent strength and purpose to their efforts to survive and even prosper. The parades and festivals which appear throughout the annual calendar of events underscore this element. While devastating hurricanes have at times inundated the land and swept away structures, they have also inspired a sense of community among the people whose resilience in the face of such hardship has gained national attention.

Biloxi: 300 Years traces the physical and socioeconomic evolution of a geographic location and its people. While maps and images reflect political and physical change, the text describes a people as they react to national economic trends or grapple with the forces of nature. Most importantly, it portrays a hospitable city on the eve of realizing its true potential, an almost two-century dream of becoming a major resort destination, a cherished label among American maritime communities.

Chapter 1

Early Biloxians

Located on the central Gulf Coast of Mississippi, facing the Mississippi Sound, Biloxi has grown in three hundred years from a sparsely settled, colonial debarkation site into a vibrant, cosmic community. Although its picturesque history mirrors that of larger regional metropolises, its location, rich marine resources, and fortuitous circumstances have made Biloxi into an emerging cultural center and resort destination.

Change came to the central Mississippi Gulf Coast early in the nineteenth century. Its annexation by the United States brought the attributes of the area before the eyes of the bustling commercial city of New Orleans. Ere long, small resorts or "watering places" emerged along the Mississippi Sound and, with Biloxi as their nucleus, became premier resorts of the "Old South." Following the Civil War, the arrival of rail transportation spurred the development of a seafood canning industry which thrust Biloxi into the mainstream of American economic life. The continued development of the seafood industry into the early twentieth century modernized the small resort town and brought it international recognition. Hundreds of immigrants poured into the town from other states and foreign countries, gifting Biloxi with an enriched cultural heritage.

Although the recorded history of Biloxi extends back only three centuries, man has inhabited or traversed the area for thousands of years. Archaeologists have encountered signs of Native American occupation throughout the Biloxi Peninsula and on nearby Deer Island. Their investigations conducted over the last quarter century along with accidental finds of artifacts and skeletal remains have provided conclusive evidence of the occupation of segments of the Biloxi Peninsula by Native American groups. Several of these confirmed sites along the periphery of the peninsula have been included on the National Register of Historic Places.

As evidence indicates, the Native American tribe with which Iberville made initial contact was not the first group to traverse the Biloxi Peninsula. As far back as the Paleo-Indian Stage, circa 14,000–12,000 B.C., wandering bands of hunters in pursuit of animal food sources traveled along the Mississippi Gulf Coast. During the Archaic Stage, circa 6000–1000 B.C., evolving coastal cultures developed techniques for extracting subsistence foods from bayous, marshes, and coastal tributaries. On the Biloxi Peninsula large quantities of oyster and clam shells have been found with bones of fish, deer, and other terrestrial and aquatic animals in Indian middens. Around 1300 B.C., some of the first Native American pottery in Mississippi appeared on the Biloxi Peninsula and at other Mississippi Gulf Coast sites. The clay was mixed with crushed oyster shell rather than plant fibers. (Walthall 1980)

Incised, decorated pottery shards and cooking balls like those above have been unearthed at various locations on both the Biloxi Peninsula and on nearby Deer Island. The arrowheads, drills, ax heads, and tools below, also found on Biloxi sites, were made from materials not native to south Mississippi and were either traded into the area by distant tribes or carried to the peninsula by migrating groups. Courtesy Edmond Boudreaux.

The Native American cultures which inhabited the Gulf Coast and lower Mississippi River alluvial valley before the arrival of the first European explorers left ample evidence of their origins. Design motifs on pottery and other materials have enabled archaeologists to identify these cultures with specific regions of North America. The elaborate Mississippian culture, a blend of numerous lower Mississippi Valley cultures, by A.D. 1000, had spread north into Tennessee, Kentucky, Indiana, and Ohio, east into Alabama and central Georgia, and southwest into Louisiana, where its contact with the counter-developing Plaquemine culture produced the Natchez and other tribes of the lower Mississippi Valley. Similarly, local finds such as arrow points indicate that the Native American groups of the Mississippi Gulf Coast were influenced by cultures which existed far beyond the Tombigbee basin and the Mississippi River/Lake Ponchartrain area. (Walthall 1980; Weber 1992)

In the early sixteenth century, the Spaniard DeSoto encountered survivors of the fading Mississippian culture which had developed westward along the Florida panhandle and across the Gulf rim. Approximately one hundred fifty years later, tribes such as the Natchez, Choctaw, Alabama, Creek, and Appalachee still exhibited vestiges of the classic Mississippian culture. The French encountered these groups migrating into the area around the mouth of the Mississippi River. By the early eighteenth century, however, European colonizers had brought an end to the Mississippian culture. (Swanton 1911)

The arrival of the French on the Biloxi Peninsula in 1699 terminated Native American presence on the Mississippi Gulf Coast. French lodgment interrupted the migration and hunting patterns of tribes whose villages lay north and west along the Mississippi River. Within three decades numerous Native American groups which had been identified by the French, located on their maps and recorded in their journals, such as the Bayogoula, Mugulasha, Koroa, Tensa, Acolapissa, and Grigra, had virtually ceased to exist. While some groups suffered as a result of intertribal warfare, still others migrated to different areas or were assimilated into larger tribes. Many simply disappeared, leaving little or no record of their forefathers who had constructed ancient temple mounds and fortified towns. The Natchez managed to survive until their revolt against and annihilation by the French in 1729. (McWilliams 1981; Kniffen, Gregory and Stokes 1987)

Although insignificant both in numbers and space occupied, the tribe for which the City of Biloxi was named, like other small tribes living along the rivers, bayous, and marshes of colonial Louisiana in 1699, is a case study for the passage of Native Americans through this period of history. Identified to Iberville by members of the Bayogoula who lived along the banks of the Mississippi River and hunted the coastal areas of the Mississippi Sound, the Bilocchy, also known as the Annochy, did not speak the Muskogean language of other southeastern Native Americans. Of Siouan stock, they were distant relatives of the Dakotas, the Crow, and the Osage, tribes inhabiting the central and northern plains, far to the north beyond the Mississippi River. The story of how this Siouan-speaking tribe, thought to be former residents of the Ohio Valley, came to occupy a small village on the Mississippi Gulf Coast, surrounded by southeastern Muskogean-speaking tribes, was lost following the chaos of European contact. The Siouan Biloxi, however, have assured their place in history by leaving a thriving city their name.

At the time of the French landing in 1699, a party of Biloxi was apparently gathering food from the peninsula and nearby Deer Island, located a few hundred yards off the eastern shore. According to Iberville's description, their village, which was actually located several miles away on the Pascagoula River, consisted of twenty long structures covered with mud and bark and completely surrounded by eight-foot-high paling about eighteen inches in diameter. (McWilliams 1981)

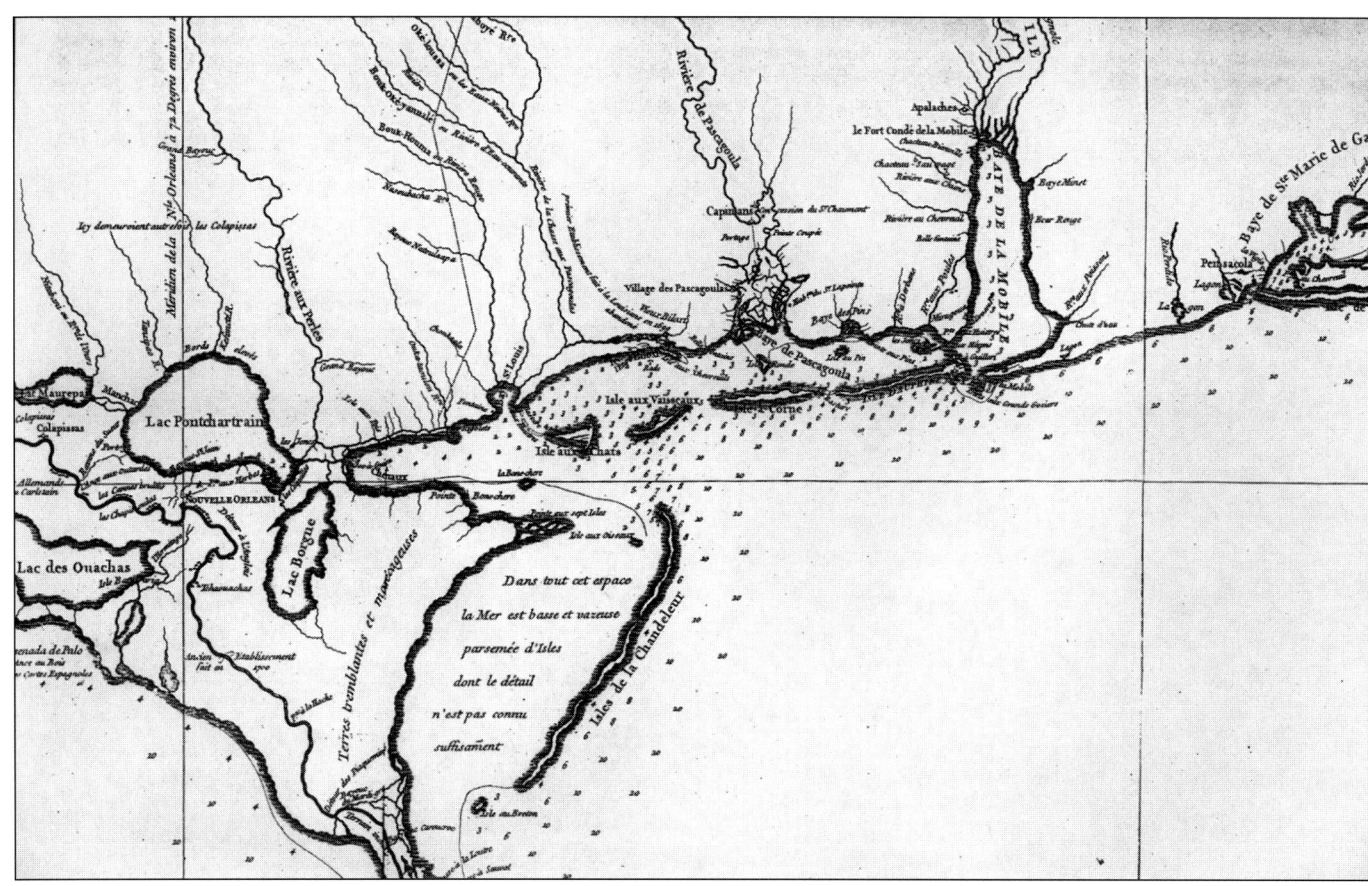

A circa 1732 French map details existing water routes and pinpoints the location of Native Americans. Place names of rivers, islands, bays, and lakes, translated into English, serve today. Courtesy Biloxi Public Library.

Drawn to the gift-giving French, the Biloxi were loyal friends, assisting Iberville in his initial ascent and exploration of the Mississippi River. When the French relocated to Mobile in 1701, the tribe followed and remained, until urged by noted explorer Juchereau de St. Denis to resettle on a small bayou behind New Orleans. In 1707 fifteen Biloxi warriors from this group reportedly accompanied the explorer on an expedition against the Chitimacha. After relocating to a site on the Pearl River formerly occupied by the Acolapissa, the tribe was reportedly back at its old Pascagoula River location in 1730. In 1763, following England's acquisition of Mobile in the wake of the French and Indian War, the Biloxi and other local Native American allies of the French migrated across the Mississippi River into Spanish territory. Most members of the Biloxi, banding with some of the Pascagoula, remained in Louisiana well into the nineteenth century. Others drifted into east Texas and settled in Angelina County along Biloxi Bayou. By the late nineteenth century, mixed groups of Biloxi, Pascagoula, and Caddoe were located along the Red River near the Texas border. Today, a small number live in the vicinity of Marksville, Louisiana. (Kniffen, Gregory and Stokes 1987; Swanton 1911; Hunter 1994)

The plight of the Biloxi was not unlike that of other Native Americans subjected to European intrusion. The wetlands Biloxi tribe had long enjoyed the bounties of the marshes, bayous, and shores of the Mississippi Sound and near-shore islands. The loss of their lands and ultimately their tribal composition and identity was harsh compensation indeed for their involvement in the global jousting of the European powers during the seventeenth and eighteenth centuries. Today, a single site on the Biloxi Peninsula pays tribute to the tribe's existence. A massive, centuries-old, live oak tree with a unique ring in one of its mighty limbs tells a tale of tribal animosities and the undying love of a warrior for a maiden.

On February 10, 1699, a small French flotilla under the command of thirty-seven-year-old Canadian Pierre Le Moyne Sieur d'Iberville arrived in the Mississippi Sound and dropped anchor in the lee of Ship Island. On February 13 Iberville set out to investigate a column of smoke rising from a small island to the northeast. Once ashore on the Biloxi Peninsula, he sighted and pursued a small party of Native Americans. His mission was the location of the Mississippi River. (McWilliams 1981)

Left: Subject of a centuries-old Indian legend, the Ring-in-the-Oak bears mute testimony to the tribe after which the City of Biloxi is named. In this 1940s image, with the historic Church of the Redeemer in the background, three visitors ponder the ring's creation. Courtesy Randy Randazzo.

Below: The early French found many similarities between the Mississippi Gulf Coast and their native Aunis, a low-lying region of salt marshes and pines in southwestern France on the Bay of Biscay. This modern image shows the entrance to the French port of La Rochelle, embarkation site of Iberville's fleet in 1698. Courtesy Veronique DePlanne.

1 Early Biloxians

Early Biloxians

The long process of discovery, colonization, and commercialization of a virtually unknown Louisiana had begun. Iberville and a handful of men in a longboat, accompanied by Bienville, his nineteen-year-old brother, and two companions in a birch bark canoe, brought the first lily-white flag of Bourbon France to the Biloxi Peninsula. Their landing was a crucial step in the rediscovery of the mouth of the Mississippi River, first located in 1682 by René-Robert Cavelier de la Salle. A military presence in the area was considered by the French crucial to the settlement and trade of western Canada and Louisiana. The Spanish were already at Pensacola, pressing toward the Mississippi River from both east and west along the rim of the northern Gulf. Moreover, the English, while driving overland from the Atlantic seaboard, had launched an expedition to the Mississippi River from England. Iberville's Canadian command contained men of proven combat experience, Canadian woodsmen or *coureurs de bois*, veterans of his 1697 Hudson's Bay campaign; Caribbean pirates or *flibustiers*; and French marines. (Allain 1988; Brasseaux 1984; Giraud 1974)

The landing of the French provides a first glimpse of the Biloxi Peninsula. On February 13, 1699, Iberville recorded in his journal that "the approach to the shore is quite shallow, half a league offshore, four feet of water. This coast runs west by south and east by north. The trees here are very fine, mixed. We are seeing many plum trees in bloom; tracks of turkeys, partridges, which are no bigger than quail; hares like the ones in France; some rather good oysters." Upon landing, Iberville discovered fresh Indian tracks which he followed east for two leagues. On February 14 he continued tracking eastward, leaving gifts at his campsite for two Indians who had been spotted observing him from a distance of three hundred yards. After walking for a league, approximately three and a half miles, he observed a canoe crossing from the peninsula to Deer Island, where five additional canoes waited. Detecting the French, the Indian flotilla fled across the mouth of Biloxi Bay. Pursuing in his birch bark canoe, Iberville followed their landing on the eastern shore and shortly made contact with breechcloth clad members of the Biloxi tribe. (McWilliams 1981; Brasseaux 1981)

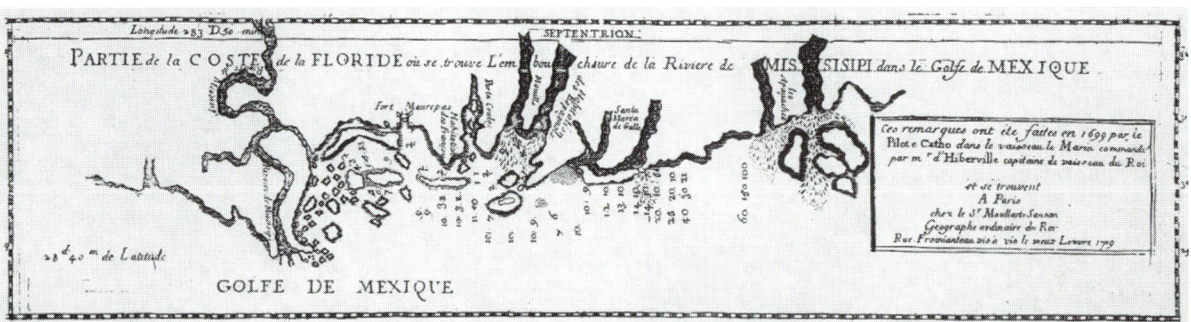

Above: This early map, drawn by Catho, pilot of Iberville's ship *le Marin*, depicts the central Gulf of Mexico coast line, including the Biloxi Peninsula. The small numbers on the map represent soundings for water depth taken by the French, who reconnoitered the coast from Pensacola to Lake Borgne in 1699. Courtesy Biloxi Public Library.

Right: The primeval landscape which greeted Iberville when he landed on the Biloxi Peninsula in February 1699 no longer exists. This view along the undeveloped south shore of Deer Island perhaps resembles what he found. Courtesy Bob Brooks.

Top: Fame, fortune, and adventure beckoned the thirty-seven-year-old Pierre Le Moyne sieur d'Iberville, Montreal-born leader of the French expeditionary force which landed on the Biloxi Peninsula. After a decade of fighting in the cold of northern Canada, this soldier of fortune responded enthusiastically to the Gulf of Mexico assignment. Courtesy Biloxi Public Library.

Bottom: Jean Baptiste Le Moyne de Bienville was nineteen when he accompanied his brother Iberville to the Mississippi Gulf Coast. After successfully exploring the lower reaches of the Mississippi, 1699–1700, he succeeded to full command of the Louisiana colony. In 1720–1722 he directed the attempted development of *Nouveau Biloxi*. Courtesy Biloxi Public Library.

Within a few days Iberville had also made contact with curious members of a hunting party of Bayogoula and Mougoulacha who lived along the banks of the Mississippi River. Several days later he set out from his Ship Island anchorage in longboats, navigating with difficulty inside the Chandeleur Islands, and on March 2 entered the Mississippi River. Much of March was spent ascending and reconnoitering the river, encountering a number of tribes along its banks. After progressing as far north as the Red River, Iberville began his return journey back to the coast by an alternate route of the Bayogoula. At Bayou Manchac he separated from the main party and made his way back with two birch bark canoes through lakes Maurepas and Pontchartrain to the original landing site on the Biloxi Peninsula. There, on March 30 he ignited a large signal fire to alert the fleet of his return. (Brasseaux 1981)

During the days following Iberville's return the French searched the Mississippi coastal area for a suitable base and settlement site. Unfavorable conditions had not permitted the establishment of a camp near the mouth of the Mississippi River. Although locating an acceptable spot on the Pascagoula River near the friendly Biloxi tribe, the French were unable to pass through oyster reefs near the river's mouth. With supplies running low, they established a base camp on the east side of Biloxi Bay and constructed a temporary fort, named Maurepas in honor of the French Minister of the Navy and the Colonies. On April 23 with the projected settlement in mind Bienville and two Canadians went to the far western end of what is now Back Bay where they found land "perfectly fine for a settlement." Progressing in a northerly direction, Iberville recorded that he "examined the backside of the little bay" with one of his Canadians and found land "very beautiful with pine woods, mixed with trees of other kinds in spots, many prairies, [and] light sandy soil everywhere." (McWilliams 1985)

> Paris, July 8. N.S. The Court is now at Versailles. It's said the Dutchess of Orleans continues her Resolution of going to make the Dutchess of Lorrain, her Daughter, a Visit. Monsieur d'Ibberville arrived on the 26th of the last Month at Rochelle from his Expedition to the West-Indies; He entred into the River Mississipi, which falls into the Gulph of Mexico, and designing to make a Settlement there, built a Fort near the Mouth of the River, and left 80 Men in it. And it's said, he intends very shortly to return thither. Our Letters from Madrid of the 18th of the last Month give an Account, that the King of Spain was present that day at the Procession of Corpus Christi; That the Price of Bread was something abated; And that the Count d'Oropesa was retired to his House at Cibola, about 18 Leagues from Madrid, and the Almirante of Castile to Granada.

On July 8, 1699, the *London Gazette* reported Iberville's expedition to the Mississippi, noting that eighty men had been left in a fort near its mouth awaiting his return. Courtesy Tim Hughes and Randy Randazzo.

Convinced that the natural qualities of the completed Fort Maurepas location would prove suitable for developing a commerce valuable to the French economy, Iberville returned to France. In between two more trips to the Mississippi Gulf Coast, he vigorously lobbied the French ministry, promoting a Louisiana colony as the barrier to English expansion beyond the Appalachians and urging that settlers be drawn from France's poor masses. In 1702, however, despite his efforts to assure the permanence of the Biloxi Bay encampment, the French transferred their operations to a location above Mobile Bay. Requiring the shipment of goods almost forty miles from the nearest anchorage, the site lacked a suitable water supply and was subject to periodic flooding and hostile Indian attacks. As in the case of the Biloxi Bay encampment, there were no settlers willing to work the soil for their own sustenance. In 1703, threatened by yet another European war, the French Crown assumed full responsibility for the Louisiana colony and increased its Mobile garrison of troops with the *Compagnies franches de la marine*. It also sent additional colonists and recruited potential wives for soldiers who wished to remain in the colony following their enlistment. (Giraud 1974)

The Mobile settlement struggled to survive for more than fifteen years. Under the governorship of Iberville's brother, Bienville, a perpetual state of starvation existed. Canadian and French factionalism threatened the peace. France's efforts to resolve problems through authority changes only worsened the situation. Between 1702 and 1715, despite France's encouragement of mercantile and proprietary ventures, the Lousiana colony's population grew little, from 140 to 215. Following the Treaty of Utrecht, which brought an end to the devastating War of Spanish Succession, France was unable to support the colony and awarded a trade monopoly to Antoine Crozat. (Giraud 1974)

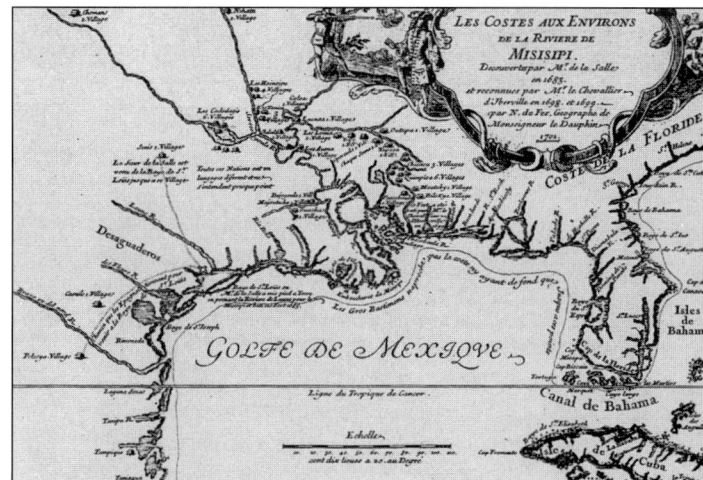

In 1701 with the French still occupying their Biloxi Bay outpost, N. de Fer pinpointed the location of the Moctobi, Biloxi, and Pascagoula tribes on the Pascagoula River as well as numerous tribes along the Mississippi River and its lower tributaries. Courtesy Biloxi Public Library.

With the death of Louis XIV in 1715, all commercial interests in the Louisiana colony were charged to Scottish financier John Law and the Company of the West. Hoping to revive a ruined French economy, Law launched an infamous promotional scheme known to history as the "Mississippi Bubble." Although advertised as a cross between the Garden of Eden and El Dorado, Louisiana failed to attract significant numbers of voluntary colonists. In desperation France legislated a policy of penal colonization, and deportation to Louisiana became a sentence for many crimes. For some French households, relocation to Louisiana meant good riddance to recalcitrant family members! (Giraud 1974)

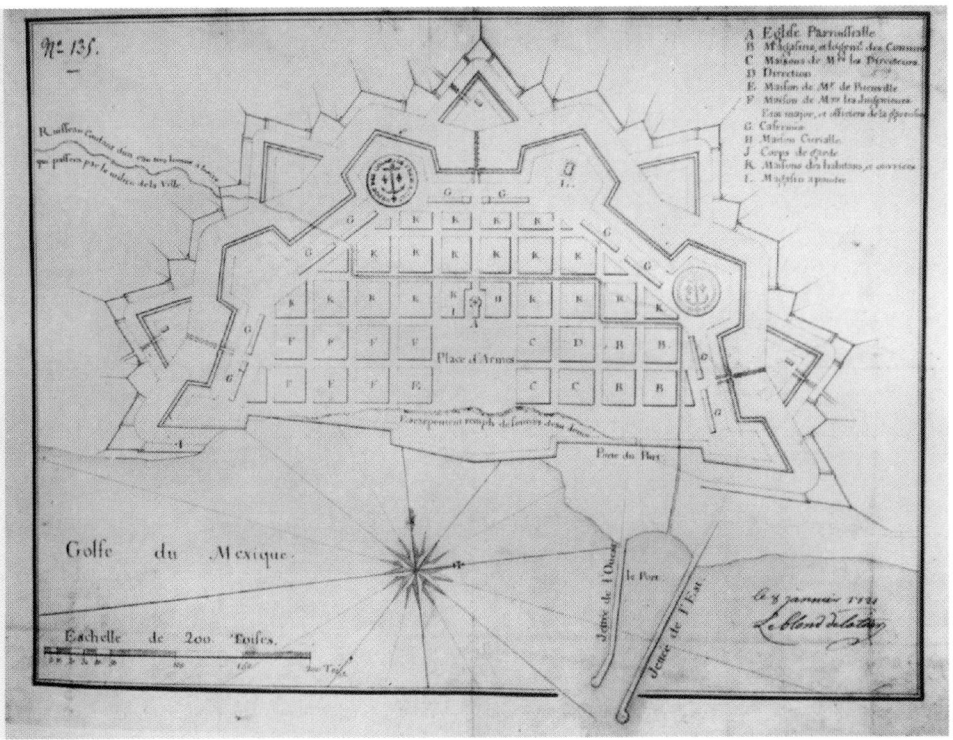

In the summer of 1718 inadequate anchorage at Dauphin Island and the threat of Spanish attack from Pensacola forced French officials to transfer operations back to the Mississippi Gulf Coast. In that same year Bienville established a new settlement on the Mississippi River, called *Nouveau Orleans*. In 1720 officials of the Company of the Indies sent employees to clear a site on the Biloxi Peninsula, north of the original deep water anchorage at Ship Island. Well-known French military engineer Leblond de la Tour arrived with his assistants and drafted a series of plans for a fortified town, called *Nouveau Biloxi*. Never used for the Biloxi Peninsula site, the plans later served as a model for Bienville's settlement on the Mississippi River. Beginning in 1720, company ships arrived with hundreds of colonists from France recruited to settle large concessions or grants in Louisiana. Temporary housing in elaborate camps greeted them. John Law, whose "bubble" had already burst, boasted an encampment which stretched along the shore of the Biloxi Peninsula facing the Mississippi Sound east of the proposed town. Short of vessels, company officials urged the rapidly increasing numbers of colonists to build their own boats for transportation to the concessions. Although more than seven thousand people arrived in Louisiana between 1717 and 1721, at least two thousand died in transit or from conditions encountered in the colony. (Conrad 1970; Mississippi Provincial Archives, French III, 281; Allain 1988)

Top: French military engineers under Pierre Le Blond de la Tour developed plans for the fortified town of New Biloxi. When the Biloxi project was abandoned in 1722, the plans were used for the settlement at New Orleans. Courtesy Biloxi Public Library.

Bottom: A variety of French artifacts, including an oil storage jar, pipe stems, gun flint, a French-style brick, and tableware shards, have been found by archaeologists on the Biloxi Peninsula, Deer Island, and in the waters of Back Bay and the Mississippi Sound. Courtesy Edmond Boudreaux.

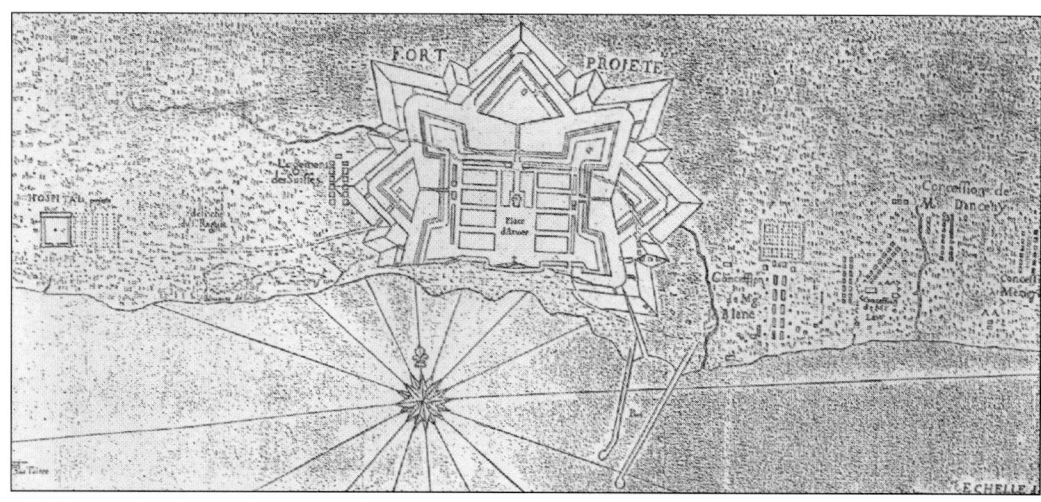

Above: This 1721 French illustration located camps of French colonists spread out on either side of the area being cleared for the fortified town of New Biloxi. Lodgings for two companies of Swiss soldier-workers and a hospital are indicated west of the fort site. Courtesy Biloxi Public Library.

Right: In December 1720 Jean-Baptiste Michel Le Bouteaux drew this image of a *magazin,* or warehouse, which was being constructed in the Law Concession at New Biloxi. Courtesy Edward Ayer Collection, Newberry Library, Chicago.

Below: Le Bouteaux also illustrated a *chaloup* under construction, among the first vessels built on the Biloxi Peninsula. A shortage of vessels forced many colonists to live for months in temporary shelters at New Biloxi while awaiting transportation to permanent sites in the Mississippi Valley. Courtesy Edward Ayer Collection, Newberry Library, Chicago.

By March 1721 company officials, workers, and engineers at New Biloxi were joined by two hundred fifty soldiers of the *Compagnies franches de la Marine*, a company of Swiss soldier-workers under the command of M. de Merveilleux; and about one hundred fifty men serving the *traversiers* which operated between Ship Island and the settlement. Including six groups of arriving colonists, New Biloxi boasted a population of twenty-five hundred. Despite intense heat and a scarcity of supplies, construction of worker's huts, carpenter sheds, blacksmith and toolmaker forges, and a chapel and hospital was accomplished. In 1722 French authorities transferred their operations from New Biloxi to New Orleans. La Page Du Pratz, overseer of plantations for the Company of the Indies in Louisiana from 1718–1734, wrote, "vessels [could] not come within four leagues of it . . . nothing could be brought from them, but by changing the boats three different times, from a smaller size to another still smaller; after which they had to go upwards of a hundred paces with small carts through the water to unload the least boats." He further noted that "a greater discouragement against making a settlement at Biloxi, was, that the land is the most barren of any to be found thereabouts; being nothing but a fine sand, as white and shining as snow. . . . There was nothing in plenty but fish [and oysters], with which this place abounds." How strange that the colony's shortcomings cited by De Pratz almost three hundred years ago have become the Mississippi Gulf Coast's most advertised attributes.

Between 1723 and 1729 French records indicate a handful of settlers and slaves at Biloxi. No military presence between New Orleans and the Pascagoula River was noted during that time. After 1731 systematic censuses were no longer taken by French authorities in Louisiana. When war erupted in 1755 between the French and English in North America, the small Biloxi settlement played no role in the hostilities. The 1763 Treaty of Paris which ended the conflict forced France to give England all of its North American holdings, except for New Orleans, which Spain received. The victorious English who examined the area reported finding inhabitants thought to be offspring of the original French settlers, raising livestock and producing pitch and tar, pursuits recommended by Bienville to colonists in an attempt to develop commerce. (Maduell 1971; Hutchins 1968)

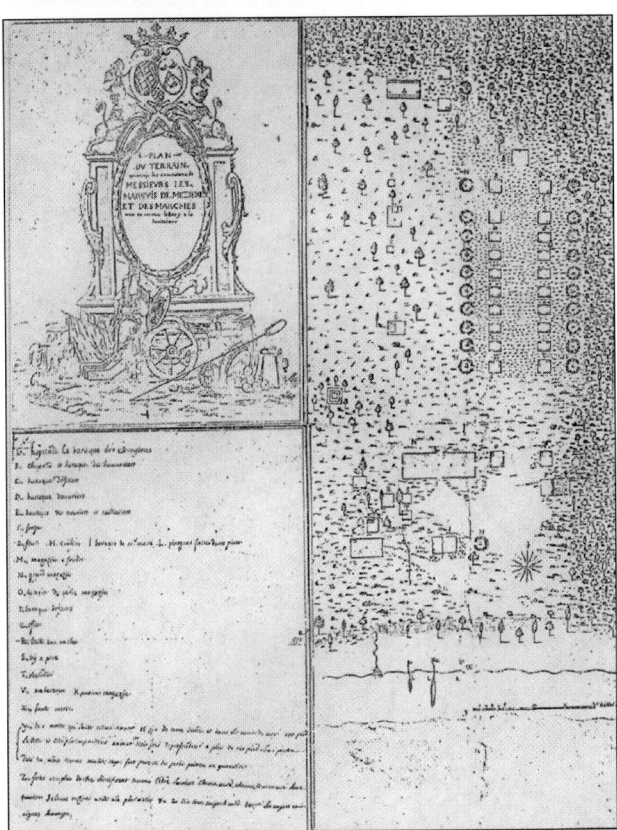

Top: This pre-Camille aerial photo shows the proposed New Biloxi site and the location of temporary encampments for French colonists. Courtesy Hinman Collection.

Bottom: This 1721 drawing of the Mezieres and Des Marches concession on the Biloxi waterfront shows two large pirogues tied to the shore. The descriptive French text notes the presence of mullet and flounder in the shallow, near-shore waters. Courtesy Biloxi Public Library.

Designating the area between Mobile Bay and the Pearl River as the County of Charlotte, the English established a military base at Mobile, garrisoned by a unit of Scottish Highlanders under the command of Major Robert Farmar. Given the task of securing the region, Farmar recommended that Biloxi be considered a possible site for one of the fortifications linking Mobile to Natchez via lakes Pontchartrain and Maurepas. In 1766 the English chose to strengthen Natchez, sending troops from the Twenty-First Fusiliers. (Claiborne 1980)

During English domination inhabitants were required to register prior land grants or claims in Pensacola by October 1764. Numerous grants were issued for rich agricultural land along the Mississippi River and around Mobile and Pensacola. Although occasionally mentioning in their journals French families living along the Mississippi Gulf Coast, English officials never expressed interest in the land. The famous English surveyor and cartographer George Gauld, charting the Mississippi Sound and Bay of Biloxi in 1768, noted that French settlers still lived in the area. Despite the fact that the British governor was authorized to grant or reward land without fee to military personnel who had served in the recent war with the French, records for the Province of West Florida listed no petitioners for acreage on the Biloxi Peninsula. The inhabitants of Biloxi and the unproductive land fronting the Mississippi Sound remained virtually isolated. (Cummins, 1993; Rea 1990; Mississippi Provincial Archives, English: 13)

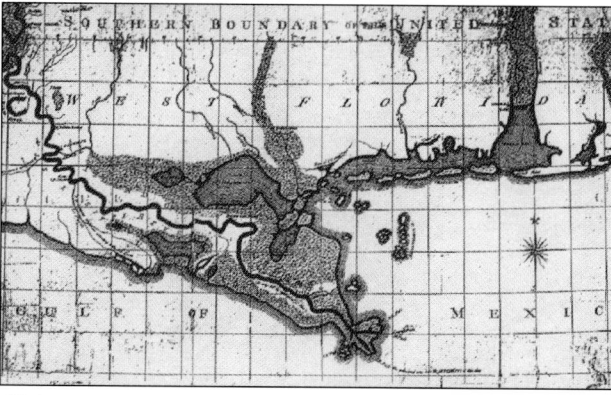

Although no settlements along the Mississippi Sound between New Orleans and Mobile are indicated on this late-eighteenth-century American map, English journals and Spanish land records note that several families of French origin occupied the Biloxi Peninsula and land along the north shore of Back Bay. The thirty-first parallel separating Spanish West Florida from the United States, surveyed by Andrew Ellicott in 1795, runs along the top edge of the map. Courtesy Biloxi Public Library.

In 1775 eruption of the American War for Independence brought no change to the sparsely settled Mississippi Gulf Coast. English presence at Natchez and nearby Mobile, however, invited military incursions by the Spanish, who entered the war in 1779 as an ally of the French. Between 1779 and 1781 Spanish forces under the leadership of Don Bernardo de Galvez, civil and military governor of Louisiana, seized the lower Mississippi River area and Mississippi Gulf Coast. The 1781 Treaty of Paris which ended the American Revolution gave the Spanish control of East and West Florida. Unable to attract colonists either from Spain or its other colonies in the western hemisphere, Spanish authorities invited immigrants from the United States to settle in the region. Generous grants of free land were offered. Settlers were required to present a written request for survey of the unoccupied parcel of land. Following the authorized survey and payment of fees, a grant was issued. Many families occupied land without waiting for the issuance of an official grant. Those families living in the region prior to Spanish takeover were only required to take an oath of allegiance to the king of Spain and the Catholic Church. (Weber 1991)

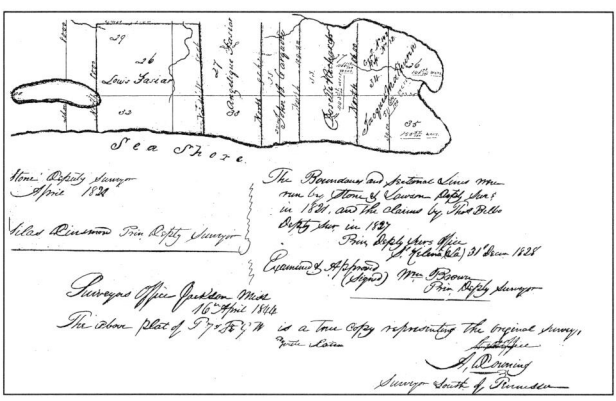

In 1821 American surveyors laying out Township Seven in Range Nine West in the District East of the Island of New Orleans and East of the Pearl River recognized acreage claims granted by the English and Spanish. This copy of the early survey shows all but the later Peytavin Claim. Courtesy Biloxi Public Library.

In 1781 grants on the Biloxi Peninsula were awarded to James Mathurin, Widow Baptiste Christian, and Nicholas Carceaux. By 1793 additional grants had been awarded, including one to Antoine Peytavin, whose lands extended from today's White Avenue west into Gulfport and north into Keesler Air Force Base. The Spanish survey of this parcel did not take place until April 1804, following the purchase by the United States in 1803 of the land below the thirty-first parallel, the northern boundary of West Florida between the Pearl and Perdido Rivers, as part of the Louisiana Purchase. (Weber 1992; Abernethy 1961)

In 1795, according to the Treaty of San Lorenzo, Spain agreed to recognize the thirty-first parallel, extending between the Mississippi and Chattahoochee Rivers, as the southern boundary of the United States. On April 7, 1798, the United States formed the Mississippi Territory with the thirty-first parallel as its southern boundary, leaving those families living on the Biloxi Peninsula in Spanish territory. In 1800, via the Treaty of San IldeFonso, Louisiana, including the Mississippi Gulf Coast, was returned to France. However, Napoleon's renewal of hostilities with Great Britain prevented the French from restoring dominion. (Prucha 1969)

Chapter 2

Americanization: Birth of a Resort

In 1802 Georgia relinquished to the United States all land between the Chattahoochee and Mississippi Rivers and between the thirty-first and thirty-fifty parallels, land which had been granted to its trustees in 1732 by King George II. On April 30, 1803, the United States purchased Louisiana from France. In addition to securing the Mississippi River, these acquisitions virtually doubled the size of the United States and temporarily satisfied the expansionist dreams of many Americans. The public domain expanded so rapidly, however, the precise boundaries became a problem. Except for the area near New Orleans, no legal boundaries were set for the vast Louisiana Purchase. Other treaties preceding the Purchase, furthermore, had set no specific boundaries for its easternmost area between the Pearl and Perdido Rivers. In 1763, following their victory over the French, the English had insisted that France cede "the river [Mississippi] and port of Mobile, and everything which he possesses or ought to possess" east of the river, except New Orleans. By the 1783 Treaty of Paris which ended the American Revolution, Spain had, in turn, required that England cede "all that she possesses to the east or southeast of the river Mississippi." In each case, the Biloxi Peninsula was included in ambiguous land transfers. (Vance 1975; Malone 1970)

Undoubtedly, few inhabitants of the Bilox Peninsula were aware of the confusion surrounding ownership of their little niche on the rim of the north central Gulf of Mexico. Following the Louisiana Purchase, Secretary of State James Madison claimed the area known as West Florida for the United States. James Monroe, minister extraordinary to France, agreed with the determination. President Thomas Jefferson adopted it as policy. In November 1803 a bill subjecting Louisiana to American law was introduced in Congress. According to the measure, navigable waters within the United States emptying into the Gulf of Mexico east of the Mississippi River were to be included in the revenue district of the Mississippi Territory which had been established in 1798. Fort Stoddard, located on the Tombigbee River well above Spanish-held Mobile, was made a port of entry. This act clearly indicated that although the United States did not physically occupy West Florida, it undoubtedly looked forward to its Americanization. (Am. St. P.: Terr. V; Cox 1918; Haynes 1952)

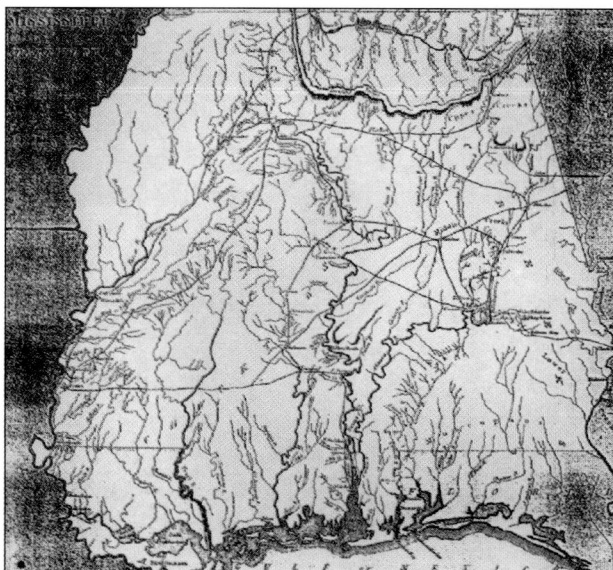

The 1798 Mississippi Territory did not include lands below the thirty-first parallel between the Pearl and Perdido Rivers. This early-nineteenth-century map depicts the later added coastal region. Early roads, trails, and areas occupied by Native Americans are noted. An absence of roads along the Mississippi Gulf Coast underscores its dependence on water travel. Courtesy Biloxi Public Library.

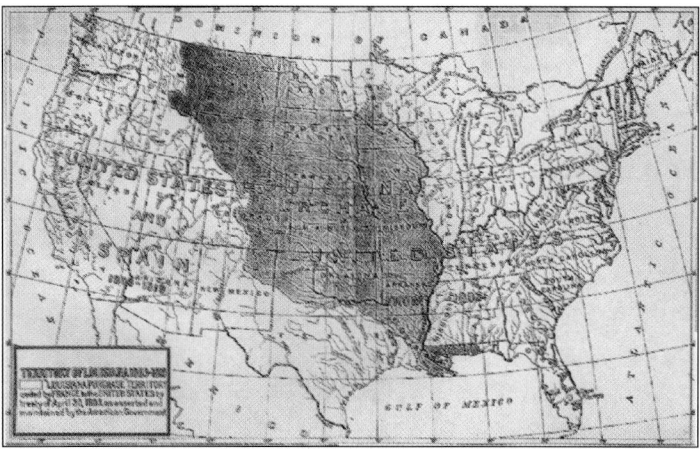

In 1803 the United States purchased Louisiana from France. This early map shows the boundaries of the purchase, ambiguously defined in the treaty as "lands formerly held or occupied by the French or Spanish" and including West Florida between the Pearl and Perdido Rivers. Courtesy Biloxi Public Library.

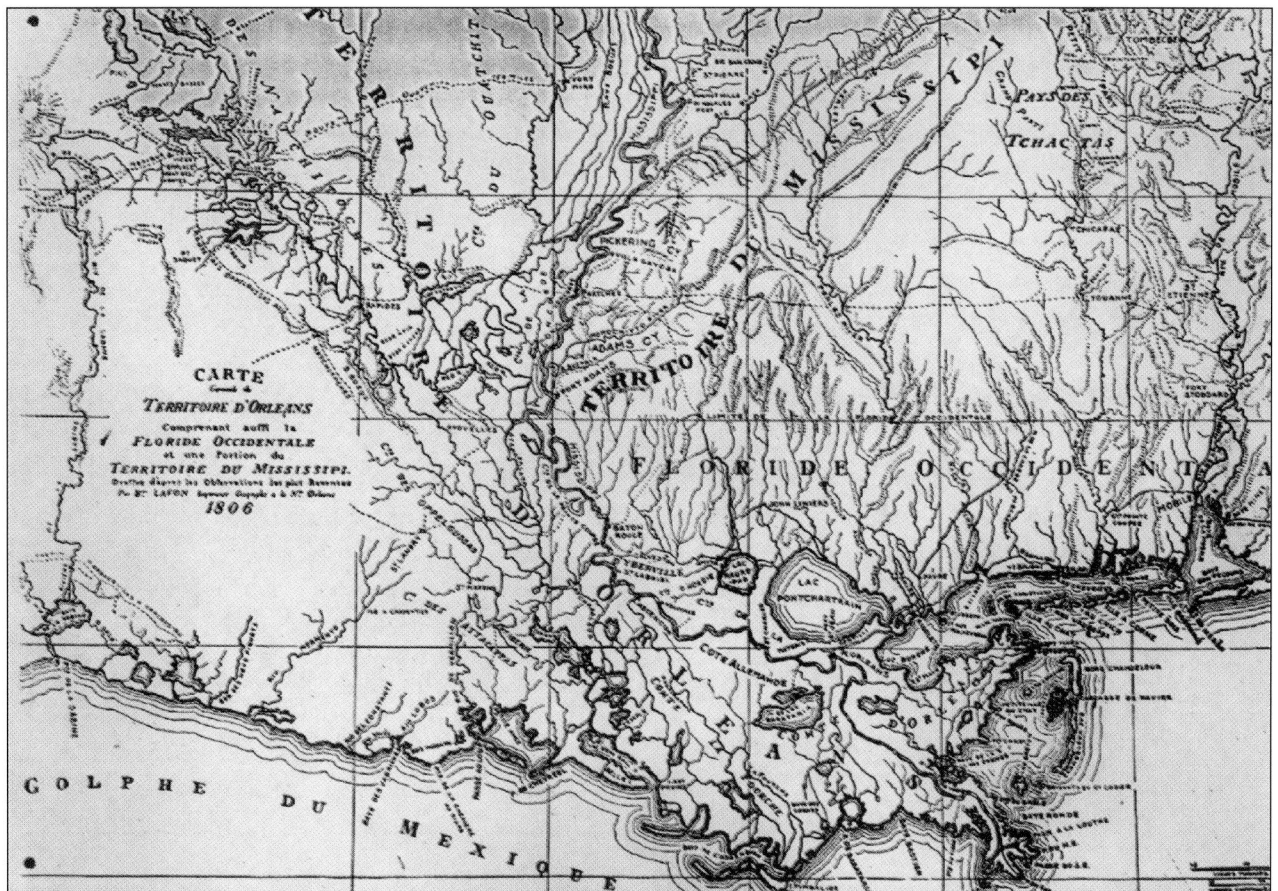

Before 1800 few English-speaking American settlers could be found along the shores of the Mississippi Sound. In 1806 twelve French-speaking families were reported living on the Biloxi Peninsula. However, Americans dominated the area around Baton Rouge and along the Mississippi River from St. Louis to the West Florida boundary. Eighty-five percent of the population of West Florida was estimated living west of the Pearl River, the majority of whom were inhabiting the rich agricultural region around Baton Rouge. The sparse number of American settlers living below the thirty-first parallel caused the United States to hesitate in asserting its claim to the land along the Gulf Coast. Its weak military presence in the region further undermined efforts to wrest control from the Spanish. In fact, legislation was enacted allowing purchase of the region from Spain. Fearing continued Spanish domination, American settlers in the area threatened insurrection. (Malone 1970; Claiborne 1980)

This 1806 map of the Orleans Territory, drawn by New Orleans architect and geographer Pierre LaFon, is one of the earliest official American maps to recognize the existence of Biloxi, the only town indicated on the Mississippi Sound. Courtesy Biloxi Public Library.

For several years following the Louisiana Purchase a lack of assertiveness on the part of the United States allowed the Spanish to continue their control of the region below the thirty-first parallel. Stiff duties were charged on American goods entering the Mississippi Territory through the port of Mobile. In 1803 the Spanish squelched minor revolts by Americans outside Baton Rouge and at St. Francisville. In 1810, however, a much larger uprising occurred. After capturing the Spanish fort at Baton Rouge, American rebels moved to eliminate other signs of Spanish authority in the province. As a result of this so-called "West Florida Revolt," the sparsely settled American area east of the Pearl River became part of an independent state known as the Commonwealth of West Florida. (Abernethy 1961; Prucha 1969; Philbrick 1965)

Although West Florida insurgents wasted no time petitioning the United States for annexation, President James Madison made no formal reply. Instead, he issued a proclamation justifying American intervention, sending instructions to W. C. C. Claiborne, governor of the Territory of Orleans, to use the few troops at his disposal to take possession of the area. By December 10, 1810, in accordance with the president's directives to organize a militia and establish a court system, Baton Rouge was garrisoned with American troops, and the newly occupied territory was subdivided into the parishes of Feliciana, East Baton Rouge, St. Helena, St. Tammany, Biloxi, and Pascagoula. (Clark and Guice 1989; Cox 1918; Ms. Terr. Arch.: Claiborne Ltr. Bk.)

On January 5, 1811, Governor Claiborne dispatched Dr. William Flood, a prominent New Orleans physician and planter, to survey the newly created Gulf Coast parishes. Sailing into the Mississippi Sound aboard the U.S. sloop *Alligator*, Dr. Flood raised American flags over the Bay of St. Louis, Pass Christian, Biloxi Bay, and Pascagoula. At each location he distributed copies of President Madison's proclamation, Governor Claiborne's ordinances establishing the new parishes, and the laws of the Territory of Orleans. He also issued Justice of the Peace commissions to a number of coast citizens, including Jacques Ladner, a resident of the Bay of Biloxi. (Ms. Terr Arch.: Claiborne Lt. Bk.; Am. St. Papers.: Terr. V; Claiborne 1980)

Upon his return Dr. Flood reported to Governor Claiborne that he found no literate inhabitants at Biloxi. "They are, all along this beautiful coast," he reported, "a primitive people, of mixed origin, retaining the gaiety and politeness of the French, blended with the abstemiousness and indolence of the Indian. They plant a little rice, and a few roots and vegetables, but depend for subsistence chiefly on game and fish." He added further that "few laws will be wanted here. The people are universally honest. There are no crimes. The father of the family, or the eldest inhabitant, settles all disputes." Flood estimated the population of Biloxi Parish, from the Pearl River to Biloxi Bay, to be 420 "chiefly French and Creole." (Ms. Terr. Arch.: Claiborne Ltr. Bk.; Philbrick 1965)

Dr. Flood's survey took him only as far as the vicinity of Pascagoula, where he found conditions much the same as at Biloxi. He had been cautioned against proceeding beyond that point for fear of encountering the Spanish out of Mobile. Entrenched in the town whose population had dwindled to an estimated three hundred, the Spanish were actively collecting exorbitant duties on goods bound from New Orleans and Natchez for American settlements along the Tombigbee River. (Weber 1992; Claiborne 1980)

Flood was "greatly impressed with [the] beauty and value" of the land fronting the Mississippi Sound. The Coast's "high sandy lands, heavily timbered with pine, and the lovely bays and rivers, from Pearl River to Mobile," he noted almost prophetically, "will furnish New Orleans [then a city of more than twenty-four thousand] with a rich commerce, and with a delightful summer resort. For a cantonment or military post, . . . this whole coast is admirably fitted." Dr. Flood's description foretold the slow but steady growth and expansion along the Mississippi Gulf Coast during the next two centuries.

When the United States purchased Louisiana in 1803, "with the same extent that it now has in the hands of Spain, and that it had when France possessed it," boundary lines were obscured. Along the Mississippi Sound ownership changes were not noted for almost a decade. Indian hostilities on its northwest frontier and attacks on American shipping by both France and England preoccupied the United States. Regardless of an obvious interest in the area, little or nothing was done to affirm American sovereignty along the Gulf rim. Signs of American authority virtually ended at the Pearl River swamps. (Louisiana Purchase, Article 1; Rowland 1978)

In the wake of secret negotiations with Napoleon, Spain declared the American purchase of Louisiana invalid. The lack of a strong American military presence in the region allowed Spanish land agents to continue business as usual. In April 1804 surveys were conducted for two large parcels of land on the Mississippi Sound which had been granted the previous spring. Since assuming control of the region in the 1780s, the Spanish had been unsuccessful in attracting colonists from either Spain or its other colonies. Consequently, Americans who took a simple oath of allegiance were allowed to settle on generous tracts of free land in both Florida and Louisiana. Furthermore, Spanish authorities did not insist that American settlers convert to Catholicism. Instead, imported Irish priests, some Spanish trained, arrived to archieve the necessary conversions. One of the two April 1804 surveys, conducted the year after the Louisiana Purchase, was for Antoine Peytavin, a French native. His tract, as surveyed by Pierre Missonet, extended from the vicinity of modern-day White Avenue westward into the Handsboro area of today's east Gulfport. (Brant 1950; Pintado Papers; Chambers 1898)

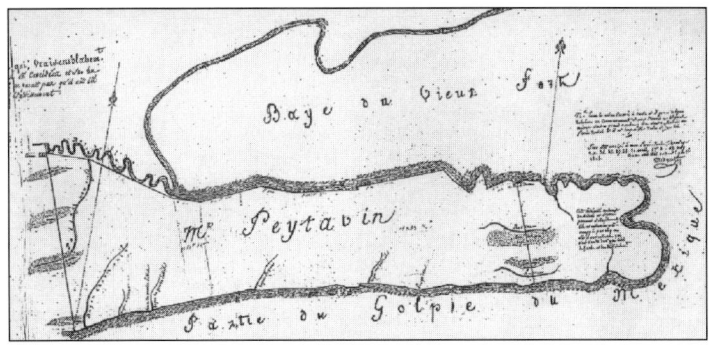

This sketch of the Biloxi Peninsula accompanied Missonet's survey report. Although the area east of the survey line is not to scale, features that exist today are identifiable. The two ravines through which his line crossed north from the Mississippi Sound to Back Bay were located just west of modern-day White Avenue. Courtesy Historic New Orleans Collection.

Missonet's survey contained a highly descriptive narrative, detailing virtually every step taken on the Biloxi Peninsula. While crossing through an area that is now the eastern edge of Keesler Air Force Base, Missonet detailed a landscape of dense pines, oaks, and palmetto; deep ravines; and swamps. No roads or trails were mentioned. Because of the task's official nature, he requested that the heads of several Biloxi area households accompany him. Longtime resident Louis Fayard, whose land adjoined the Peytavin tract, along with Philippe Saucier, Pierre LaFontaine, Claude Ladner, and Andre Durocher served as witnesses to the marking of trees, the only system available on the peninsula at that time for separating two claims. The east side of major trees along the survey line was marked LF/M, while the west side was marked AP/M, the initials of the landholders and the surveyor. (Pintado Papers)

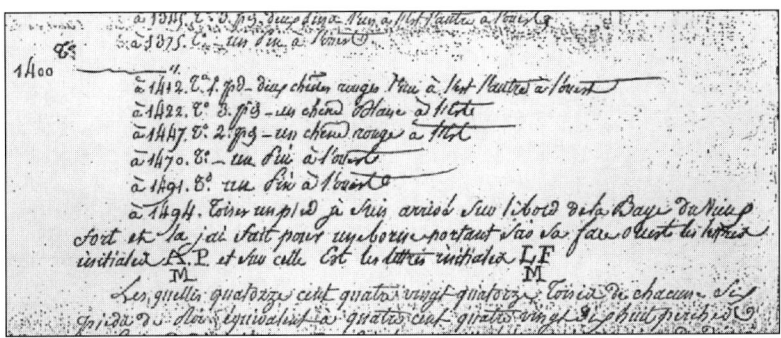

An April 1804 survey of the dense Biloxi Peninsula by Pierre Missonet was written in French and included these entries. Courtesy Historic New Orleans Collection.

The Peytavin claim and those of other earlier Biloxi Peninsula grantees, including Louis Fayard, Angelique Fayard, John Carquotte, Dosette Richards, and Jacques Mathurin, were laid out using the arpent, nearly an acre in size, as a standard measure. Frontages were almost exclusively on navigable rivers, streams, and bayous. When acreage was subdivided during the early nineteenth century, the use of long riverine lots and arpents continued. In Biloxi early property lines often ran from the Mississippi Sound due north to Back Bay, more than a mile in some places. (Cassibry 1986)

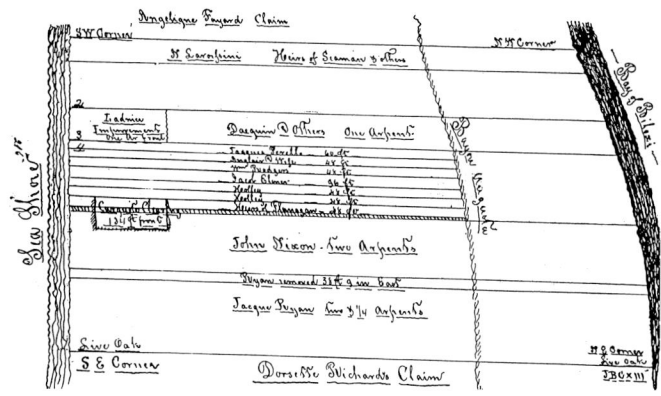

The "long lots" seen on this early map were typical of the property boundaries found on the Biloxi Peninsula during much of the nineteenth century. The divisions indicated here lay between the Dorsette Richards and Angelique Fayard claims. Two live oaks were used to mark the terminus of the western boundary of the Richards claim. Harrison County Records.

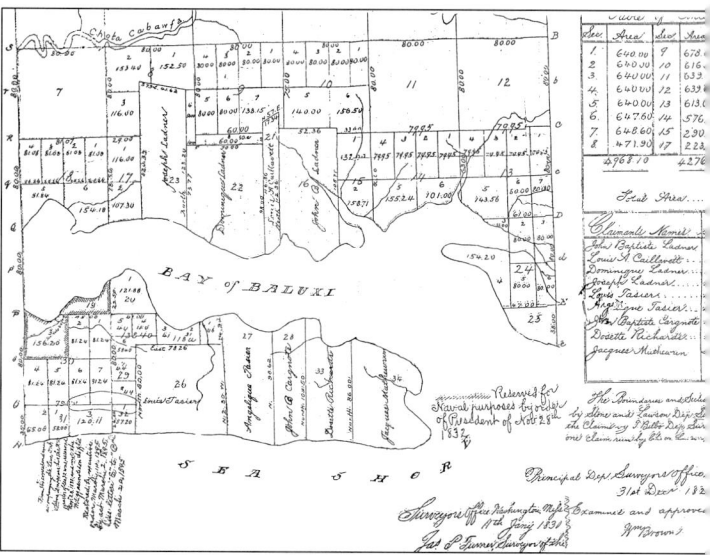

In the early 1820s surveyors from the United States Land Office in St. Helena noted few unclaimed properties on the Biloxi Peninsula. This Land Office map shows several sections on the western peninsula, mostly within the unlisted Peytavin Claim. Courtesy Biloxi Public Library.

At the time of the Peytavin survey President Jefferson was seeking to dispense with off-size acres and statute miles whose rationales were buried deep in English history. In the former English colonies an irregular system of metes and bounds surveying was used, producing a crazy quilt of property lines that invited future land litigation. Familiar with the system, however, many Americans resisted the change. Nevertheless, the public domain was laid out using the square mile, easily divisible by a surveyor's chain. As early as 1785 government surveyors had begun laying out a framework for organized settlement beyond the Ohio River and by 1796 had instituted a system of ranges containing six-mile-square townships divided into 640-acre sections. A series of north-south meridians and intersecting baselines provided initial points for township surveys and usually preceded actual settlement. By 1803 these meridians had reached the Mississippi Valley. (Garrett 1988; Cotterill 1930; Carstensen 1976)

The line of the thirty-first parallel between the Mississippi and Chattahoochee Rivers became the base line for official United States surveys on the Mississippi Gulf Coast. Surveyed in 1799 by Andrew Ellicott, this line was the southern boundary of the United States, separating it from Spanish Florida. Federal surveys effected after the creation of the United States General Land Office in 1812 placed the sparsely settled Biloxi Peninsula in Township Seven, Range Nine West, in the District West of the Island of New Orleans and East of the Pearl River. Because of the westward movement of its city limits, the western portion of modern-day Biloxi lies in Range Ten, whose dividing line with Range Nine lies in the vicinity of Iberville Drive. (Claiborne 1980; Gallalee 1965)

In addition to laying out the public domain, early federal surveys identified all land not previously claimed through French, English, or Spanish grants. The local survey disclosed that little unclaimed land remained on the eastern half of the Biloxi Peninsula. When those claims predating the Louisiana Purchase were later certified by federal survey, most fell within, or were adjusted to, the 640-acre maximum allowed under the Land Act of 1796. After these claims had been applied to the township map, remaining parcels were identified for sale as part of the public domain. In 1850, in a deposition given during a court case involving one of these early claims, seventy-three-year-old Elihu Carver commented that, as a deputy United States Surveyor in 1822, he had found that none of the residents on the Biloxi Peninsula possessed Spanish grants or any other written proof of title to the holdings. It had been common practice for early Biloxi settlers, he learned, to sell or exchange claims with no written legal proof. (Cassibry 1986; Sec. St. Rec.: RG 28)

In December 1810 Mississippi Territory delegate George Poindexter presented a bill to the United States Congress providing that the Territory of Orleans, including West Florida, be admitted to statehood. Fearing the creation of too large a state, Congress amended the bill to exclude the West Florida parishes. In April 1812, shortly before declaring war on Great Britain, the United States welcomed Louisiana into statehood, recognizing the Pearl River as its eastern boundary below the thirty-first parallel. Despite its reluctance to take any action that might prejudice future negotiations for Florida, the United States annexed the region between the Pearl and Perdido Rivers to the Mississippi Territory. The newly annexed region, called Mobile County, included the settlement of Mobile which was still garrisoned by the Spanish. In December 1812, although fearful of Spanish-sponsored Indian attacks on American settlers, Governor David Holmes petitioned the Mississippi Territorial legislature to subdivide Mobile County into two counties, Hancock, which included the Biloxi settlement, and Jackson. In April 1813 an American force under General James Wilkinson forced the surrender of Mobile, allaying all fears of Spanish reprisal. (Abernethy 1961; Rowland 1978)

Before the War of 1812, the United States showed great concern over the vulnerability of New Orleans and the recently annexed Gulf Coast region. Left unguarded, the area beyond the Pearl River offered an overland avenue to New Orleans. Supplied by British and Spanish agents operating from Pensacola and the Florida panhandle, hostile Indians plagued the region. With his successful military campaign to subdue Indian activities in the region, General Andrew Jackson, commanding a force of regular Army troops, Tennessee volunteers, and territorial militias of Louisiana and Mississippi, propelled the United States into direct conflict with the English and Spanish in Florida. (Prucha 1969; James 1933)

In 1813 the British in North America targeted potential allies in the Gulf region. Included were local Indian tribes, such as the Creeks, already at war with the Americans; disaffected Frenchmen, Spaniards, and Blacks; and a small group of Baratarian pirates. Initially the English planned to land at Pensacola, march overland to Mobile, and advance through West Florida to a point above New Orleans. In the summer in 1814, reinforced by veteran army and naval forces following Napoleon's defeat, the British moved into Spanish Pensacola. However, in November they were ousted by American forces under Jackson. Choosing a more direct route to New Orleans, British forces anchored in the waters off Ship Island, twelve miles south of the Biloxi Peninsula, planning their assault through Lake Borgne and the swamps east of the city. On January 8, 1815, following a series of engagements that had begun in mid-December with a naval encounter off Bay St. Louis, the English under the command of General Edward Pakenham, decorated veteran of many Napoleonic encounters, were soundly defeated by Jackson and his cosmopolitan American forces at the historic Battle of New Orleans. (Rowland 1978; Mahon 1972)

During the time of the New Orleans campaign, the isolated, awkward terrain along the coast of the Mississippi Sound, laced with shallow bayous and streams, encouraged the construction of few roads. Overland transportation was virtually unheard of. As early as 1804, a year after postal service had been extended to New Orleans, the regional surveyor Isaac Briggs reported that few roads existed in the area below the thirty-first parallel. The two-hundred-mile journey to New Orleans from Fort Stoddard, the United States customs station on the Tombigbee River above Mobile, required up to twenty-five days hard travel. Traversing the piney woods above the settlements on the Mississippi Sound, the postal carrier followed the route south to the lower Pearl River where he boarded a schooner for the trip to New Orleans. In 1806 fear of the Spanish forced the United States to authorize construction of a more direct route along the thirty-first parallel known as the Federal Road. (Cain 1953; Lang 1932; Sullivan and Powell 1985)

On the eve of the War of 1812 the general westward movement of settlers into the Public Domain, known as the Great Migration, swelled the population of the Orleans and Mississippi Territories. Several years earlier, United States Land Offices had opened at St. Stephen's, located on the Tombigbee River ninety miles above Mobile, and at Washington, capitol of the Mississippi Territory, near Natchez. Although large regional sales of land were projected, actual sales were disappointing. By 1808, with the continuing Spanish presence at Mobile, less than ninety-five hundred acres had been sold. In the district east of the Pearl River, which included the Mississippi Gulf Coast and Biloxi, few sales were recorded. During the period of the West Florida Revolt, 1810–1811, hostile Indians and rumors of Spanish invasion in the isolated counties of the lower Tombigbee Valley discouraged settlement. Along the Mississippi Gulf Coast, no sales were recorded. (Cottrill 1930; Lowery 1968; Owsley 1945; Am. St. P.; For. Rel. 2)

In 1812 Louisiana's statehood fueled renewed interest in the rich land along the Pearl River. More than 120,000 acres were sold. Annexation of the two Gulf Coast counties to the Mississippi Territory, likewise, drew settlers from Georgia and the Carolinas. The United States Census of 1820 recorded the population of Hancock County, which included all of present-day Harrison County, as 1,594. (Bureau of the Census 1820; Philbrick 1965; Walters 1969)

As a result of postwar migration, south Mississippi and the Gulf Coast counties welcomed emigrants from the poorer districts of Georgia and the Carolinas. However, the same sandy soil that had thwarted the French and failed to attract either English or Spanish settlement in the eighteenth century aroused little interest in those accustomed to raising herds of livestock or cultivating rice, corn, tobacco, or cotton. The two water-oriented Gulf Coast counties did not share the agrarian interests which carried Mississippi to statehood in 1817. Their economies maintained close ties with the populations of New Orleans and Mobile.

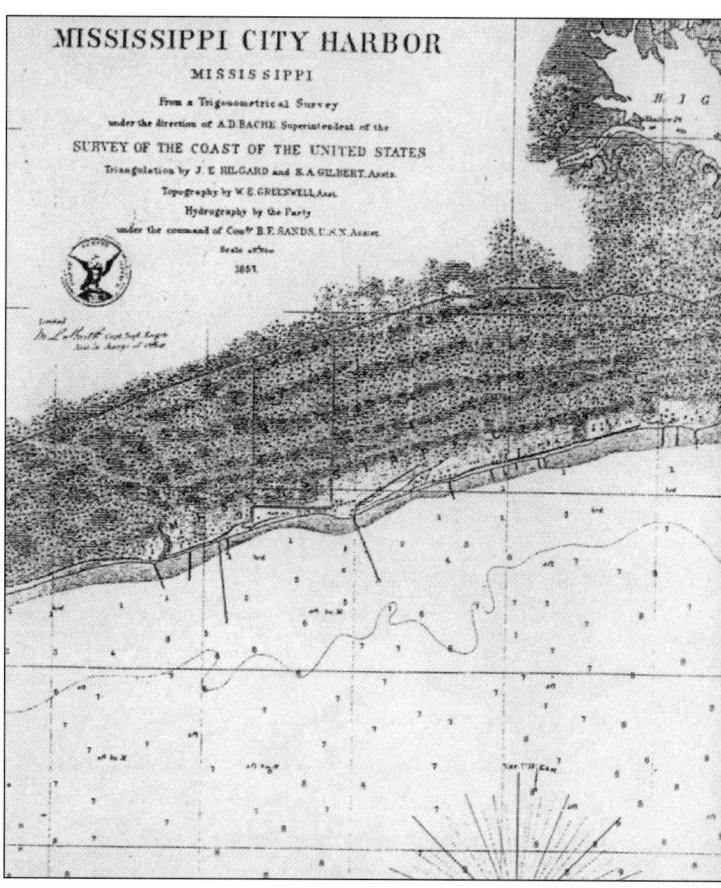

This 1857 Coast Survey map of Mississippi City Harbor includes the western portion of modern-day Biloxi and its significant land features. The Pass Christian–Point Cadet Road, a bayou emptying into the Sound from behind Beauvoir, and a stream at today's Porter Avenue are easily recognized. Courtesy Biloxi Public Library.

In the 1820s wealthy businessmen and planters from New Orleans, seeking to trade the summer ills of the city for the seafood and cool, salty breezes of the Mississippi Sound, began erecting homes and summer cottages along its shores. Small villages sprang up, and the numbers of fishermen, boat builders, merchants, hotel keepers, truck farmers, and others increased. Shieldsborough, Pass Christian, Biloxi, Ocean Springs, and Pascagoula were soon popular "watering places" of the Mississippi Sound. The few pioneer families of the Mississippi Gulf Coast were joined by a rapidly expanding population.

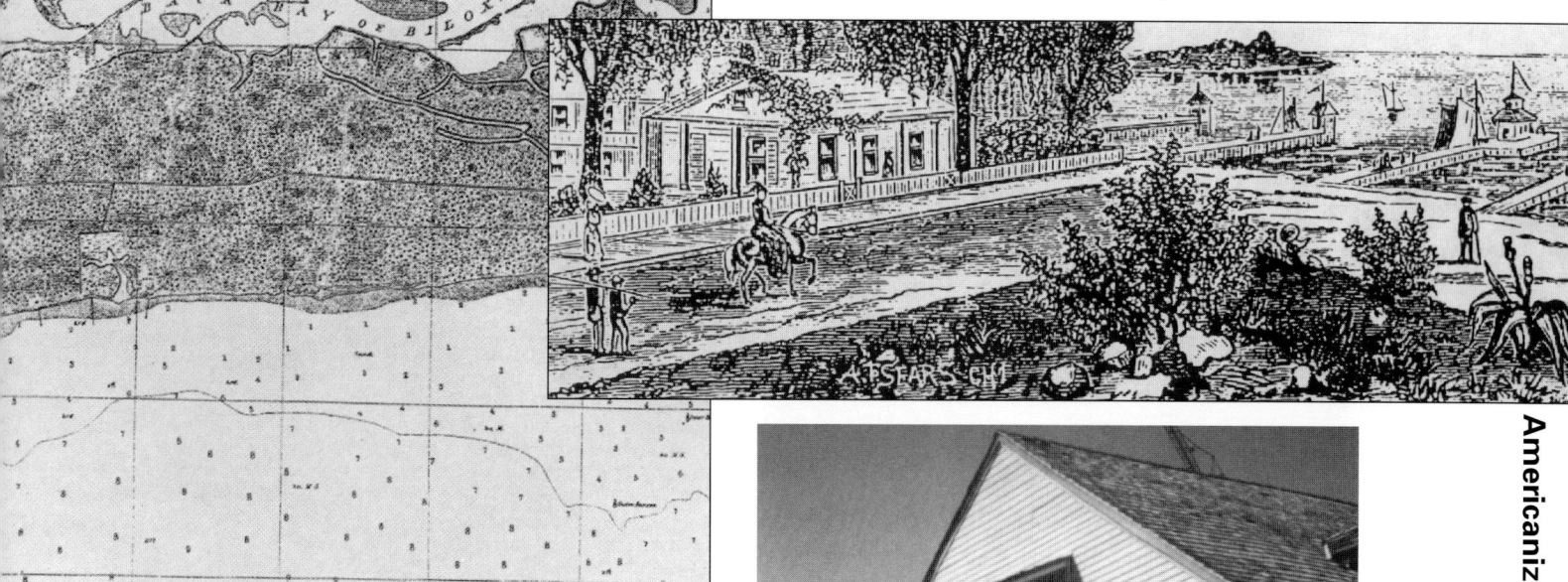

In the 1830s, as New Orleans families sought to escape seasonal onslaughts of yellow fever, the number of dwellings along the Mississippi Gulf Coast began to multiply. Within a short time daily steam packets began serving the coastal area and the town's population swelled. Encouraged by the popularity of the Mississippi Gulf Coast, entrepreneurs developed plans for a new port and rail terminus, called Mississippi City, which they hoped would rival New Orleans. By 1841, business and political interests had wielded sufficient power to create a new coastal county, Harrison, named after recently elected President William Henry Harrison of the War of 1812 fame. The new county extended from the Bay of St. Louis to Biloxi Bay with centrally located Mississippi City as its seat. Rumors of port and railroad development stimulated the growth of the adjacent industrial village of Handsboro, which bustled with lumber mills, brick works, foundries, and boat works. Although water transportation was easily available, a network of roads between the two extremes of the county was developed to provide access to the more isolated shoreline summer residences and to link the ancillary businesses with the small resort communities which they serviced. An early coastal pathway became the Pass Christian–Point Cadet Road, today known as the Pass Road. (Lang 1921; Bureau of the Census 1840, 1850)

Top: Built in 1847 by John Hohn, the Magnolia Hotel was one of Biloxi's premier antebellum hostelries. This postwar woodcut presents an idealized view of the hotel and its detached kitchen-dining room. In the background are Deer Island, numerous piers and sailing vessels, and an arriving steamboat. Courtesy Biloxi Public Library.

Bottom: The only remaining antebellum hotel on the Mississippi Gulf Coast, the Magnolia Hotel was relocated and restored by the City of Biloxi following Hurricane Camille. Today the hotel houses the Mardi Gras Museum and offices of the Gulf Coast Carnival Association. Photo by the author.

Americanization: Birth of a Resort

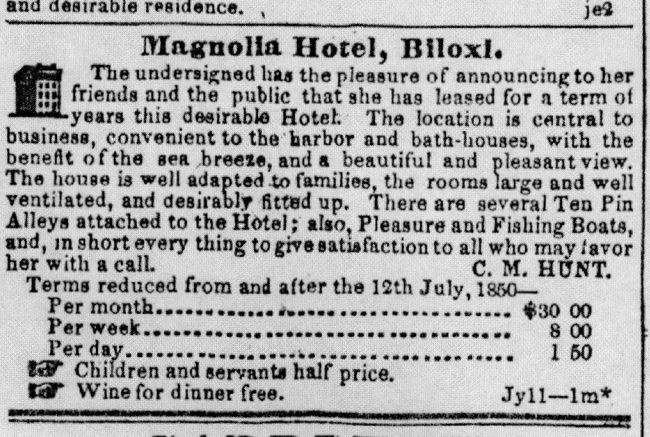

Top: This 1850 Magnolia Hotel ad from the *Daily Picayune,* designed to attract New Orleans families, touts the hotel's convenient location and numerous amenities. Courtesy Maritime and Seafood Industry Museum.

Above: During the antebellum period numerous Biloxi hotels advertised in the *New Orleans Daily Picayune*. The Green Oaks Hotel, located near the Toledano House on East Beach, boasted its own company of fishermen and oystermen in this July 1850 ad. Courtesy Maritime and Seafood Industry Museum.

Biloxi's antebellum tourist trade was dependent upon the steamboat. This 1850 *Daily Picayune* column advertises several of the packet steamers which serviced the Mississippi Gulf Coast's watering places. Some of the same vessels later served the Louisiana Navy during the American Civil War. Courtesy Maritime and Seafood Industry Museum.

During the 1840s the Mississippi Gulf Coast emerged as a major antebellum resort. Easily accessed by inexpensive steamboat transportation, its "watering places" lay undisturbed by the American war with Mexico. Chartered as a town since 1838, Biloxi boasted a permanent population of nearly six hundred, most of whom resided in a small area about a mile wide and several blocks deep, midway on the south side of the peninsula. The town's growth attracted a number of permanent church groups. In 1842, after decades of service by itinerant priests, a Catholic parish was established. The same year a Methodist group was organized, followed by the Baptists in 1845 and the Episcopalians in 1849. Sawmills, brickworks, and boatyards dotted the shoreline of Back Bay, and by decade's end, numerous hostelries, including the Biloxi Hotel, the Magnolia Hotel, the American Hotel, the Shady Grove Hotel, Pradat's Hotel, and the Bachelor's Hall, lined the waterfront. Along with schedules for numerous packet steamers, their advertisements were found in leading newspapers. The *New Orleans Daily Picayune*, the *New Orleans Daily Delta*, and the *New Orleans Crescent* beckoned tourists to the little resort town. An 1847 ad of the Green Oaks Hotel printed in the *Daily Picayune* read, "Mrs. Pradat has engaged a company of fishermen and oystermen to provide the hotel with the several varieties of Fish, in abundance, such as Redfish, Trout, Croakers, Pompano, Spanish Mackerel, Crabs, Shrimps, & c." The same ad listed other amenities, including a barroom, billiard tables, a yacht and sailboat, bathing houses for both men and women, and separate accommodations for families. A similar 1850s ad by the same hotel boasted the addition of a 144-foot-long ballroom. (Jones 1956; *New Orleans Daily Picayune*, July 29, 1847, Sept. 2, 1850)

Erected in 1848 and long a favorite subject of artists and photographers alike, the Biloxi lighthouse guided vessels to the town well into the twentieth century. This late-nineteenth-century railroad advertisement shows the light with its oil house and keepers quarters. The one-story Robinson-Maloney house is on the right. Courtesy Randy Randazzo.

In 1848 the United States Lighthouse Service erected the Biloxi lighthouse on the western edge of the little resort town. Its unique telescoping cast iron sections were fabricated in Baltimore by Murray and Hazelhurst Vulcan Works and shipped to Biloxi aboard the brig *Governor North*. Assembled upon a brick foundation and lined with locally made brick, the Deep South's first cast iron lighthouse boasted a fifth order Fresnel lens and nine brass lamps. Perhaps the city's most enduring symbol, the Biloxi Lighthouse guided the area through a period of tremendous growth. At midpoint in its three hundred-year history, Biloxi experienced a burgeoning population. Deadly outbreaks of mosquito-borne yellow fever in New Orleans swelled the summer crowd into the thousands. In June 1853, however, an infected New Orleans visitor brought the virus with him. By October Dr. Andreas Byrenheidt, a local physician, had recorded 533 cases and 111 deaths. (MacKenzie 1967; Lang 1932; Sullivan and Powell 1985)

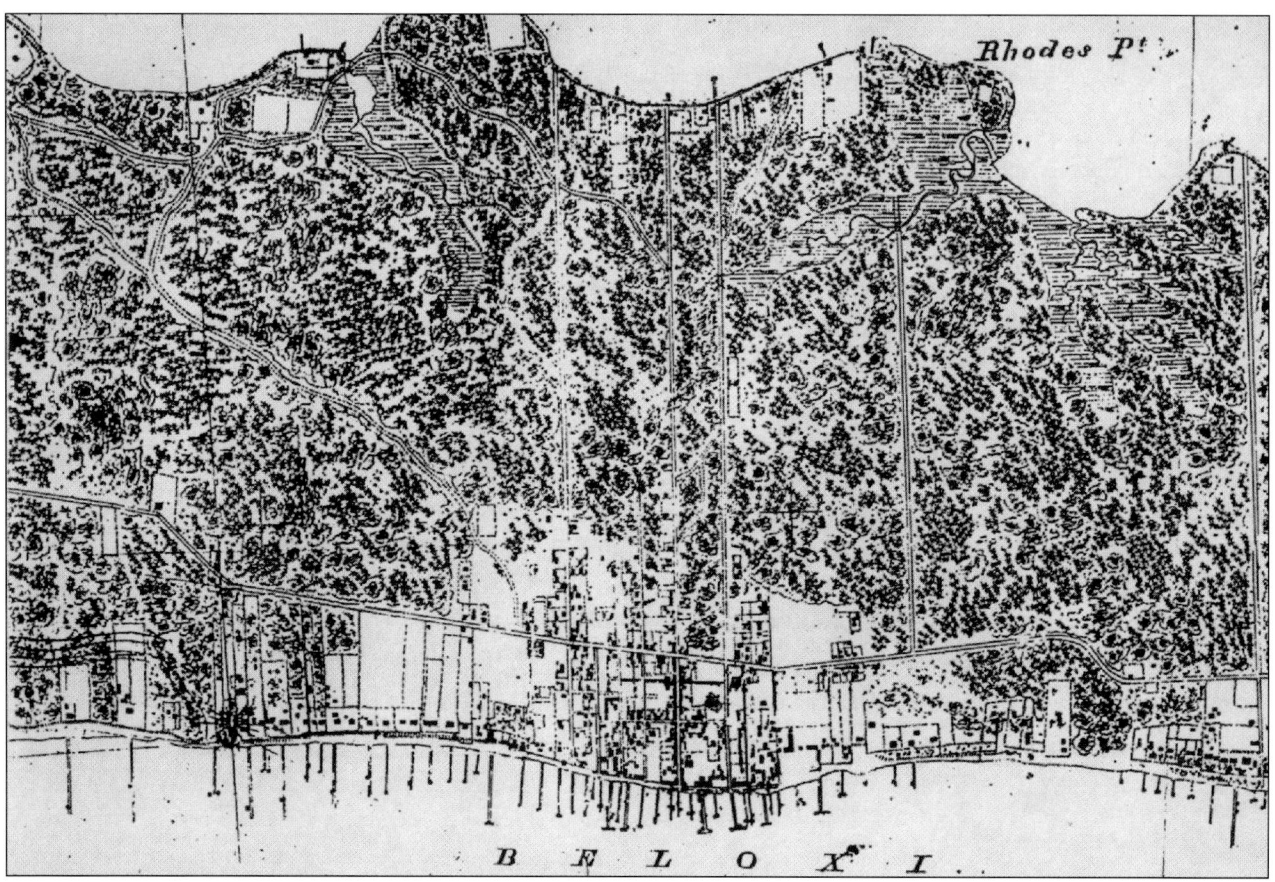

The Coast Survey which mapped the Mississippi Sound, 1848–1853, provides an amazing view of Biloxi midway in its 300-year history. Closely packed buildings easily identify Lameuse Street as the town's primary thoroughfare. Courtesy Maritime and Seafood Industry Museum.

During the 1850s the United States Coast Survey, forerunner of the Coast and Geodetic Survey, produced several maps of the Mississippi Gulf Coast. One series of sheets, drawn between 1848 and 1853, detailed every foot of the Mississippi Gulf coastline between the Pearl and Pascagoula Rivers. The entire Biloxi Peninsula, with its countless piers and bathhouses jutting into the Sound, its new lighthouse, and a dense Lameuse Street business district, was impressively captured by the surveyors. The closest thing to an aerial photograph, the meticulously illustrated maps showed the location of every pier, building, road, trail, and terrain feature. The Biloxi town limits at the time were Bellman Street to the east and Caillavet Street to the west. (U.S. Coast Survey: Biloxi 1851)

On August 25, 1852, the Mississippi Gulf Coast was struck by a major hurricane. Benjamin Wailes, an assistant professor of geology at the University of Mississippi, was in Biloxi at the time conducting an agricultural and geological survey of the state. He recorded in his journal that the area was raked by a hurricane which "raged with unabated violence throughout the day . . . tearing off the branches, and mutilating the live oaks and magnolias," and leveling several houses. Props had to be used to prevent a long, two-story boarding complex adjoining the Biloxi Hotel where he was staying from collapsing. Two days later, riding across the peninsula, Wailes noted a number of small watercraft in Back Bay. Several others had been beached and were undergoing repairs. He also viewed the Kendall Brick works, visible across the bay, several steam-powered sawmills, and a steam ferry operating from the foot of Lameuse Street. He mentioned meeting Dr. Byrenheidt, who gave him a French copper coin, dated 1721, which had been excavated in his garden. Leaving a crippled Biloxi on August 28, Wailes noted that he was forced to travel slowly because the Pass Road was strewn with pine trees felled by the storm. (Wailes 1852)

By 1860, despite its popularity as a resort, Biloxi's physical inventory included few brick buildings and a primitive road system. Virtually all transportation was by watercraft, steam packets, schooners, cat boats, sloops, luggers, and skiffs, and any hauling in the town was reportedly done with three dumpcarts. The town's principal commercial landing was at the south end of Lameuse Street in front of the Shady Grove Hotel, today the site of the Biloxi Visitors Center. Low-pressure steam packets disgorged visitors, mail, and merchandise daily at the Lameuse Street Wharf. (Lang 1932)

The two cottages flanking the main residence on the tree-shaded grounds of *Beauvoir* are shown in this turn-of-the-century view. The east cottage, foreground, was rented by Davis when he began to write his *Rise and Fall of the Confederate Government*. **Courtesy Randy Randazzo.**

Constructed in 1856, *Beauvoir* became the last home of Confederate President Jefferson Davis. In 1877 while working on his memoirs, Davis rented one of its cottages from owner and admirer Sarah Dorsey. Although purchasing *Beauvoir* in 1879 for $5,500, Davis made no payment before inheriting all of Ms. Dorsey's property upon her death. This view by artist Marty Wilson depicts Davis' *Beauvoir*. Courtesy of the artist.

According to the Eighth United States Census, 1860, Biloxi's population at the close of the antebellum period numbered approximately nine hundred. Data collected from each household indicated that 28 percent of its inhabitants were foreign born, with the largest numbers coming from Germany, Ireland, and France. Other nationalities represented were Spain, Switzerland, Italy, England, Scotland, Austria, Belgium, Denmark, Sweden, Mexico, Russia, Canada, and Norway. Few mid-nineteenth-century American towns could boast of such foreign heterogeneity. Furthermore, 25 percent of the town's population had migrated from twenty-three other states, especially neighboring Louisiana and Alabama. The balance of the town's population recorded its birthplace as Mississippi. (Bureau of the Census 1860)

Top: Constructed in 1856 by New Orleans cotton broker Christoval Toledano and later owned by Garner Tullis, the Toledano House is one of Biloxi's links to the antebellum South. This pre-Camille view from the east features the magnificent, legendary Councilor Oak, one of the Mississippi Gulf Coast's oldest. Courtesy Scholtes Collection.

Bottom: Following Hurricane Camille, the Toledano House was purchased and restored by the City of Biloxi. Today it is one of the City's premier historic sites, offering visitors a unique glimpse into the mid-nineteenth-century. Photo by the author.

This early shoreline view east of the lighthouse features the Biloxi waterfront as it looked during much of the second half of the nineteenth century. With lumber cheap, virtually every waterfront home had a pier. Courtesy Randy Randazzo.

During late summer of 1860 three hurricanes raked the Mississippi Gulf Coast. The September 14 storm altered the shoreline and virtually destroyed the Biloxi waterfront. The Biloxi lighthouse with its foundation undermined was left leaning precariously. Hundreds of tourists from New Orleans, impatient to leave Biloxi's devastation, caused a furor when an arriving steamer refused to provide immediate escape. As a result, the parent New Orleans and Mobile Mail Line Company temporarily discontinued service, and the refugees were forced to seek passage from landings in neighboring Mississippi City and Ocean Springs. (Sullivan and Powell 1985)

Although the official uniform of Mississippi State troops called for a frock coat embellished with red trim, the Biloxi Rifle Guards copied the uniform worn by the Jefferson Davis' Mississippi Rifles during the Mexican War—a red shirt and white cotton duck trousers. Courtesy Edmond Boudreaux.

During the antebellum decades Biloxi had developed a true resort economy. Strengthened by the rapid growth of neighboring New Orleans, the nation's second largest seaport in 1860, whose culture and ethnicity it reflected, Biloxi had become one of the Old South's true resort destinations. The American Civil War, however, brought great change to the area. In 1859 John Brown's raid at Harper's Ferry, Virginia frightened southern communities into organizing militia or defense companies for protection. Biloxi formed the Biloxi Rifle Guards, commanded by John D. Howard, Mexican War veteran and local businessman. Uniformed in white cotton trousers and red shirts similar to Jefferson Davis' Mississippi Rifles of Mexican War fame, the group drilled at its armory on Lameuse Street and took rifle practice off a Back Bay beach. (Howell 1991, Lang 1932)

On January 9, 1861, Mississippi became the second Southern state to secede from the Union. A few days later, in possibly the state's first hostile act, a contingent of Biloxi Rifles and Handsboro Minutemen seized the only Federal military facility in the state, an unfinished fort on the west end of Ship Island. Considered critical for the maintenance of communications between New Orleans and Mobile, the fort was occupied by Confederate forces. In March, however, following President Lincoln's order for a blockade of the South's coasts, elements of the Union Navy began patrolling the Gulf of Mexico. In June the screw steamer U.S.S. *Massachusetts* arrived in the Mississippi Sound to secure Ship Island and intercept local shipping. During one episode a detachment from the *Massachusetts* used a captured schooner to trap local trading schooners on the west end of Deer Island. With Federal forces in the Mississippi Sound, Mayor James Fewell ordered the removal and concealment of the Biloxi lighthouse lens. Although lighthouse keeper Mary Reynolds complained vehemently to Mississippi Governor John J. Pettus, the light remained extinguished for more than five years. (Howell 1991; MacKenzie 1967)

In September 1861, the Union naval presence in the Mississippi Sound forced the removal of Confederate troops from Ship Island. At Pass Christian, however, local companies were mustered into regiments, forming a brigade of the Army of Mississippi. The Biloxi Rifles became Company E in the Third Mississippi Infantry. Part of Featherston's Brigade in Loring's Division of the Army of Tennessee, this regiment would participate in campaigns throughout Mississippi, Georgia, Tennessee, and the Carolinas. Names such as Champion Hill, Kennesaw Mountain, Peachtree Creek, Franklin, Nashville, and Bentonville would long be remembered by Biloxi veterans.

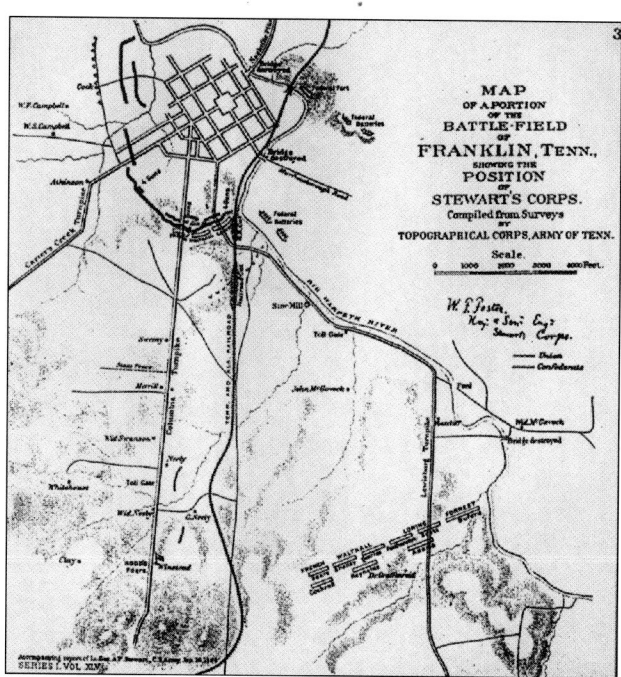

The Third Mississippi Infantry participated in numerous campaigns and several major battles during the course of the Civil War. At the Battle of Franklin, Tennessee on November 30, 1864, the unit lost heavily while deployed on the extreme right flank of the Army of Tennessee. Official Records of the Union and Confederate Armies.

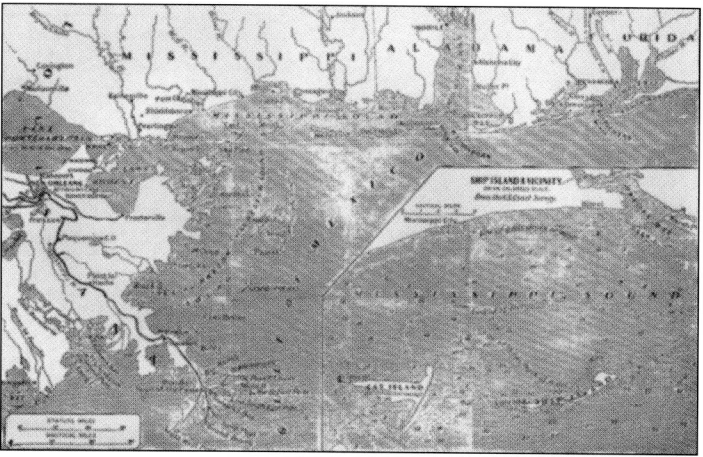

Occupation of Ship Island and its natural deep water harbor along with control of the Mississippi Sound were critical to the successful Union assault on New Orleans, the South's largest city. This period map shows the road network which linked the Mississippi Gulf Coast's watering places with that river port and the rest of the South. Courtesy Biloxi Public Library.

With the Union Navy in undisputed control of the Mississippi sound, the Third Mississippi Infantry and a host of other units were sent to bolster Confederate defenses in Kentucky. Anticipating Farragut's spring 1862 assault on New Orleans, Union troops on Ship Island, including members of the Coast Survey, continued to multiply. On New Year's eve, an armed force from the island landed and captured Biloxi without firing a shot. The Union naval officer in charge reported finding the town "almost deserted by male population." All activity took place near the lighthouse, where a battery of two rusted guns recently dredged from Back Bay along with logs painted black to resemble cannon had for weeks kept Federal forces at bay. During this landing a Northern war journalist accompanying the Union forces reportedly had a conversation with a local resident who proclaimed that the only way to starve Biloxians into submission was to put a blockade on mullet! Thus was coined the term "Biloxi Bacon." (Official Records, Navy: 1, XVII; Rebellion Record: III; Howell 1991; Lang 1932)

Increased Union activity in the Mississippi Sound precipitated the return of the Third Mississippi Infantry to the Mississippi Gulf Coast. For a short time following their return, the oystermen and fishermen from the Biloxi company were deployed from Back Bay to patrol the Mississippi Sound in an armed steam launch borrowed from the Confederate Navy at Mobile. On April 2, 1862, five hundred men from the Ninth Connecticut Infantry landed in response to gunshots fired from a mob on the Biloxi waterfront at a grounded Union schooner which had been delivering a young shipwreck survivor under a flag of truce. After cutting telegraph lines and looting the store of a suspect, the Federal forces departed. Two days later, several companies of the Third Mississippi Infantry moved toward Biloxi. While Confederate units were marching east along the narrow, sandy Pass Road, Federal forces attacked the Third Mississippi Infantry's base camp above Pass Christian, driving off a portion of the regiment left as a guard and capturing one of its flags. A short time later, Confederate authorities transferred the Third Mississippi Infantry to Louisiana to bolster defenses at New Orleans. The men in the Coast companies did not return home until 1865. (Howell 1991; Official Records, Army: VI; Dufour 1960; Rowland 1978)

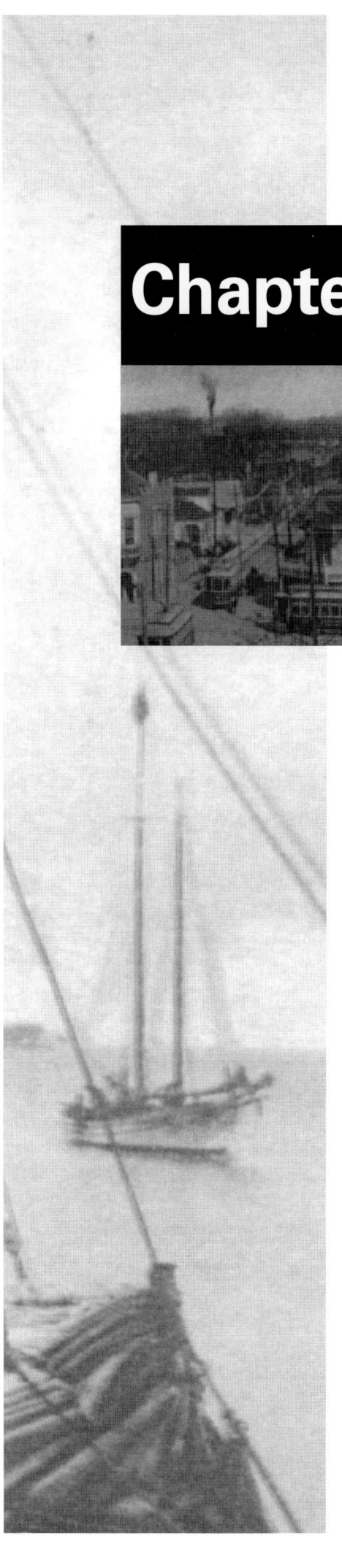

Chapter 3

Birth of a Modern City

Despite early war boasts that Biloxians could survive by eating mullet, one Union Navy commander, who landed at the town during the final weeks of the Civil War, generously distributed all of his ship's stores to the starving populace! The oystermen and fishermen who returned to Biloxi following the war found their families destitute and piers and boats in need of repair. Many returning Confederate veterans and their families survived on wild game from fields and forests. Biloxi's men harvested the bounties of the Mississippi Sound. By the fall of 1865 the timber industry was recovering and steamboat service had resumed. However, few New Orleanians could afford a summer respite in one of the Mississippi Gulf Coast's newly opened hotels. As a result, the Biloxi economy languished. (*New Orleans Times*, June 8, 1865; Howell 1991)

Biloxi's entry into the economic mainstream of the United States hinged upon the development of rail connections with large markets. This postwar map shows Biloxi's isolation prior to the construction of the New Orleans to Mobile rail link. Official Records of the Union and Confederate Armies.

In 1867 Congressional Reconstruction designated the Mississippi Gulf Coast as part of the Fourth Military District under the direction of General E. O. C. Ord. In that same year surveyors marked the right-of-way for the New Orleans, Mobile, and Chattanooga Railroad. Within two years population figures for the three Mississippi Gulf Coast counties reflected the presence of hundreds of laborers who were busily preparing the line's roadbed and constructing trestles over bays, bayous, and marshes from the Rigolets to Pascagoula Bay. In November 1869 track laying began on the line which was projected to link the great port of New Orleans with the east and New York via Atlanta. One year later regular freight and passenger service was being offered between New Orleans and Mobile. As a result, coast lumber mills relocated and truck farming developed. Steamboat travel between Mobile and New Orleans declined rapidly. (Ninth U.S. Census, 1870; Coulter 1947)

An early arrival on the railroad from New Orleans in 1870 was William H. Foster, who recommended the purchase of a large tract of waterfront land west of the town to the New Orleans Felicity Methodist Church for use as a church campground. This early image shows the Campground's tranquil waterfront and several of its cottages. Courtesy Randy Randazzo.

The construction of a railway depot between Reynoir and Caillavet Streets caused a shift in business development from the waterfront to the Pass Christian–Point Cadet Road, today's Howard Avenue. In this pair of turn-of-the-century images, wagons await arriving passengers and freight. Stands of pine in the undeveloped area north of the railroad are visible above. Courtesy Randy Randazzo.

The arrival of the railroad precipitated an increase in the number of visitors to Biloxi. Connections via New Orleans and Mobile with other lines feeding from northern metropolitan areas revived the town's hope of becoming a year-round resort destination. The greatest number of visitors, however, still came from the prosperous and burgeoning Crescent City. Among these in early 1870 was William Foster, a New Orleans lawyer and member of that city's Felicity Methodist Church. The beauty of the Biloxi seashore led him to recommend the purchase of a large tract of land just west of the town's limits for use as a Methodist campground. The parcel was owned by wealthy New Orleans soap maker and major Biloxi landowner J. H. Keller. The 1870 selling price for its 114 acres, which extended from the waterfront north to the Federal Naval Reserve on Back Bay, was only $1,400. A 1919 timber harbest in the area north of the railroad would bring $8,750, and during the land boom of the 1920s, investors would offer a whopping $750,000 for the parcel. Except for a few shorefront homes and a segment of the old Fayard grant which had been deeded to Biloxi in the 1840s for use as a cemetery, the land beyond the Biloxi lighthouse lay undeveloped prior to the 1870 sale. By the late 1890s the Camp-ground site had become a popular rendezvous and sometimes refuge for families seeking to escape frequent Gulf Coast yellow fever epidemics. More than eighty cottages and meeting structures occupied the grounds between the railroad and the Mississippi Sound. In the 1890s an eight block parcel of Keller's property along the shore east of the campground and beyondthe town's limits became one of the earliest western subdivisions. Keller Street, which bisected the parcel, was later renamed after the so-called "poet-priest of the Confederacy," Father Abram Ryan, a sometime Biloxi resident and occupant of a shore side home which today still bears his name. (Chalmers 1937; Lang 1932; Harrison County Deeds 1870; Harrison County Chancery Court Records, Book 72; Coulter 1947)

Top: This view shows one of the Campground's large, open air meeting facilities. Virtually all structures at the Campground were oriented to take advantage of breezes coming from the Mississippi Sound. Courtesy Alan Santa Cruz.

Middle: As this early 1904 image shows, the waterfront west of the Campground remained primitive, with scattered oak, pine, and palmetto along the shore. Courtesy of Randy Randazzo.

Bottom: By 1906 the rails of the Mississippi Coast Traction Company reached beyond Beauvoir and joined those being laid east from Gulfport. This early image shows its freshly laid tracks with the Campground grocery in the background. Courtesy Randy Randazzo.

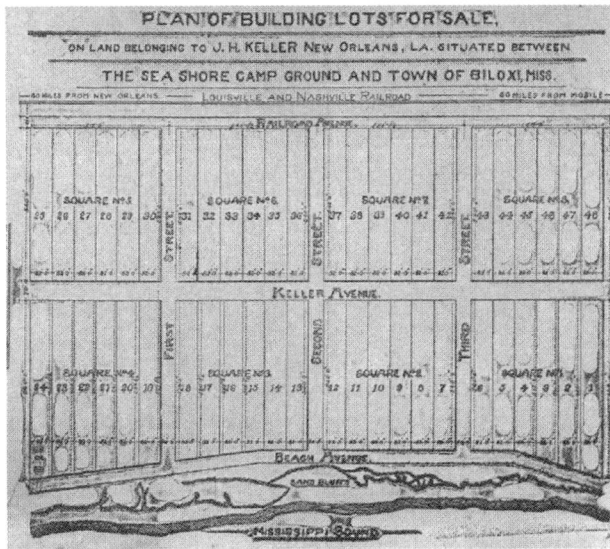

The combination of railroad and trolley service stimulated interest in Biloxi real estate. This ad from the March 30, 1895 *Herald* offers lots for sale in Keller Subdivision just beyond the town limits. Keller Avenue, one of few Biloxi streets with a New Orleans-style neutral ground, would later become Father Ryan Avenue. Courtesy Biloxi Public Library.

The construction of a railroad depot between Government, renamed Fayard, and Reynoir Streets prompted the relocation of numerous businesses. Prior to 1870, the main commercial district had stretched along south Lameuse Street, terminating at the town's primary entry wharf. After that time, businesses sprang up near the new railroad depot and along the nearby Pass Christian–Point Cadet Road. Land sales also increased, especially for waterfront property. Historically large parcels were subdivided to accommodate New Orleanians seeking to build summer residences, and a small truck farming industry emerged just west of town along the Pass Road. During the later part of the century the construction of suburban railroad stations at Beauvoir, Seashore Campground, and Gill Avenue stimulated Biloxi's westward expansion.

Top: The advent of the railroad spurred growth along the waterfront west of the lighthouse. This image shows numerous summer residences with their white picket fences lining the shore in that quarter. Courtesy Alan Santa Cruz.

Bottom: The most imposing waterfront structure west of the lighthouse was the White House. The former residence of Judge W. A. White was renovated and converted into a luxury hotel which served visitors until the post-Camille period. Courtesy Alan Santa Cruz.

Birth of a Modern City

Top: This 1915 view of the Gulf from the front lawn of the W. A. White residence shows one of the city's early trolleys. The motorman can be seen standing at the controls on its open deck. The arched oak remains today on this historic property. Courtesy Alan Santa Cruz.

Bottom: This 1920s view of the Gulf from the "veranda" at the White House shows a new two-lane road, tennis courts, a fountain, and an enhanced pier. Courtesy Randy Randazzo.

By far the railroad's most significant impact on Biloxi was its role in the creation of an internationally prominent seafood industry. The lack of rapid transportation and a reliable means of preservation had long stymied the commercialization of the Gulf Coast's most plentiful natural resource, seafood. Biloxi fishermen had oversupplied local markets for years. In 1867, however, the Dunbar family began the canning of shrimp in New Orleans. About this same time New Orleans companies began the production of inexpensive, artificially made ice. By 1870 that hot, humid city had become the South's principal ice producer, averaging seventy-two tons daily! Soon after the railroad's arrival on the Gulf Coast, small quantities of ice-packed oysters were being shipped several hundred miles inland. Responding to a national demand, many Atlantic seaboard communities also began shipping oysters to large inland towns and cities. (MacKenzie 1996)

For more than half a century the workhorse of the Biloxi oyster industry was the Biloxi schooner. This rare action photo shows a schooner crew trimming sails and winching a dredge-load of oysters onto the deck. Their captain, Johnny Simmons, far left, oversees the action. Simmons Family image, Joe Scholtes Collection.

Above: In this early image oysters are being laboriously unloaded from a schooner near the foot of Lameuse Street. Rough sawn planks protect the deck from being scared by oyster shells. A water cask sits amidst oysters piled against the cabin. Courtesy Maritime and Seafood Industry Museum.

Below: Although oyster reefs surrounded the Biloxi Peninsula, the most bountiful lay off Pass Christian and the fringes of Lake Borgne. This unique aerial view shows two Biloxi schooners working a reef somewhere in the west Mississippi Sound. Courtesy Maritime and Seafood Industry Museum.

In 1880 a group of Biloxi entrepreneurs, with little or no experience in seafood canning, formed a company and set out to construct the town's first seafood "factory." After studying Baltimore's bustling oyster canning operations and securing equipment, William K. M. Dukate, a railroad ticket agent from Indiana, along with Gulf Coast natives F. William Elmer and William F. Gorenflo, English-born John Maycock, and postwar Spanish immigrant Lazaro Lopez, opened a seafood processing plant on Biloxi's Back Bay. After their initial success, the partners dissolved the company and set up rival operations. Competition for quality and production in the seafood industry led to the development of a number of Biloxi enterprises. By mid-decade with the national oyster boom increasing demand, plants had opened at locations along Back Bay, on Point Cadet, and in five neighboring Mississippi Gulf Coast towns. (Sheffield and Nicovich 1979; Harrison County Deed Book 9; Dyer 1896)

In the mid-1880s technology aided the industry's growth. An improved oyster dredge, called a "drudge" by local fishermen, was a triangular iron device with a tooth bar which was dragged across the oyster reefs by a sailing schooner. The oysters were raked into a heavy knitted cord bag attached to the dredge, which was then laboriously retrieved by a hand-cranked winch. More efficient than hand tonging, the device permitted the rapid harvest of oysters from much deeper waters. In 1887 Biloxi's own Artesian Ice Company began producing artificially made ice. Delivered to the docked schooners by wagon, the ice was used in the shipping of oysters. During shrimp season, sawdust from local lumber mills was used to insulate iced catches of shrimp, permitting the fleet to remain in the Gulf for longer periods. (MacKenzie 1996)

Top: In this view taken just after the turn of the century near the old Biloxi Yacht Club, oysters are being unloaded from a schooner while a host of other vessels lie anchored in the calm waters of the Biloxi Channel. Deer Island lies in the distance. Courtesy Randy Randazzo.

Bottom: This 1905 image shows the hectic activity at a cannery on Point Cadet where schooners often sailed up to factory piers, using their centerboards as a brake. Courtesy Scholtes Collection.

FINE SCHOONER IS COMMISSIONED

Marjorie D. Built by Jack Covacevich is Twin Vessel to William Ewing, Recently Launched.

Biloxi, Feb. 2.

The Marjorie D., a fine new schooner fifty feet long, owned by Mrs. W. K. M. Dukate, has been finished and placed in commission. It was constructed by Jack Covacevich at his ship yard on Back Bay and will be placed in the service of the Dunbars, Lopez & Dukate Company.

This schooner is a twin to the William Ewing, which was launched a few months ago and placed in the service of the same company. Both schooners are as fine as any in the fisheries service on the coast and are material additions to the fleet of this big packing company.

Had Time Enough.

Barber—Hair's going gray, sir. Little Binks—Expect it is. Haven't you nearly finished?

The launching of a Biloxi schooner was often reported in the *Daily Herald*. This notice appeared in a 1914 issue. The *Marjorie D.*, approximately fifty-three feet on deck with an eighteen foot beam, was still listed as a sailing vessel in 1930. Courtesy Maritime and Seafood Industry Museum.

In the 1880s challenge races between returning oyster schooners led the Biloxi Yacht Club to sponsor an annual schooner race, featuring the top schooners and their captains from each cannery. The traditional Fourth of July race continued until the 1930s, attracting thousands of onlookers. This 1920s view shows six of the "white-winged queens" racing out into the Mississippi Sound. Courtesy Scholtes Collection.

The true workhorse of local factory fleets was the famous Biloxi oyster schooner. Sloops and single-masted New Orleans luggers, so named because of their unique, dipping lug sail reminiscent of eighteenth- and nineteenth-century French fishing vessels, also plied the waters of the Mississippi Sound. The versatile schooner, however, which had been used during the antebellum period for both fishing and hauling timber and freight, was still a local favorite. Broad of beam, with a shallow draft and a powerful complement of six sails, these two-masted, gaff-rigged vessels fished the waters of the Mississippi Sound and Louisiana marshes. Often referred to as "white-winged queens" by local sailing afficionados, these locally built schooners were used in combination with Biloxi skiffs to deploy seines during shrimp season and to dredge oysters. By the 1890s with its six to seven man crew, the Biloxi schooner was almost single-handedly responsible for carrying the town to prominence as the "Seafood Capital of the World." Each Biloxi factory employed its own small fleet of the town's namesake vessels. During oyster and shrimp seasons, the Mississippi Sound and adjacent Louisiana marshes were filled with schooners, their decks awash with overabundant catches, racing back and forth between factory and reef. Friendly challenges between captains returning with their catches evolved into one of the area's major tourist attractions, an annual Fourth of July schooner regatta. In 1888 the best captain and schooner from each factory competed in a fifteen-mile triangular race. For decades enormous crowds flocked to the Biloxi waterfront for this annual event. When Mississippi lifted its ban on the motor-harvesting of oysters in the early 1930s, the schooner's sails were removed. (Holt 1968; Husley 1993; Sheffield and Nicovich 1979)

Top: This rare image from the 1920s shows two crew members shucking oysters on the deck of a schooner sailing in the Mississippi Sound. Above their heads flies the schooner's clubfooted jib. Courtesy Maritime and Seafood Industry Museum.

Bottom: Early Biloxi seafood canneries shared similar architectural features, such as picking sheds, warehouses, boiler rooms, and boat ways. This early postcard view shows a typical cannery with its boiler stacks jutting skyward and schooners moored at its piers. Courtesy Randy Randazzo.

Top: Filled oyster cars like those in this early view were pushed into iron steam boxes inside a factory. Following the steaming process, the cars were quickly surrounded by groups of shuckers called oyster car gangs. Courtesy Alan Santa Cruz.

Bottom: For almost a century oyster houses were a common sight along the Biloxi waterfront. In this view shuckers are busy filling their pails outside the Clark Oyster House on Central Beach. Courtesy Alan Santa Cruz.

Top: For decades a common sight on the piers which extended into the Sound from Biloxi factories included a long row of cars loaded with tons of oysters waiting to be rolled into steam boxes inside the factory. Courtesy Maritime and Seafood Industry Museum.

Bottom: In this rare shipboard image taken somewhere off Biloxi, two young, barefoot crew members pose at the helm while two others finish a meal. Courtesy Maritime and Seafood Industry Museum.

By 1890 Biloxi canneries employed almost twenty-five hundred workers, more than twice the town's population two decades earlier. Their numbers were not sufficient, however, to process the total seasonal harvests. Immigrant labor transported by rail from Baltimore swelled the ranks of the workers well into the 1930s. Called Bohemians by the local press because of their association with the unwieldy Austro-Hungarian Empire, the Poles and Austrians had an economic impact on local businesses. Their arrival and departure was often front page news in Biloxi's primary newspaper, the *Daily Herald*. Adding considerable flavor to Biloxi's already cosmopolitan population, two other major groups supplied manpower to the seafood industry during its formative years. "Cajuns" from southwest Louisiana parishes were brought by train to work in Biloxi factories during times of critical labor shortages. Part of the massive wave of more than seven million eastern European immigrants to the United States, Yugoslavians from the Dalmatian coast of the Adriatic, escaping the turmoil of continuing ethnic divisiveness in the Austro-Hungarian Empire, found Biloxi with the aid of New York immigration authorities. (Schmidt 1995)

In 1911 the noted photographer Lewis Hine, while working for a Senate subcommittee investigating child labor, captured poignant images of immigrant workers inside Biloxi canneries. In this view workers are gathered around an oyster car which sits on rails beneath a single hanging light bulb. Courtesy Biloxi Public Library.

Top: In this Lewis Hine image immigrant workers pose outside a Biloxi cannery. Some still hold the large tin oyster cups which were hooked onto the side of the oyster car and used to measure the output of shrimp or oysters. Courtesy of Biloxi Public Library.

Bottom: Notwithstanding whitewashed walls, factory interiors were stark. This poignant Lewis Hine image captures the coarse ambiance of a Biloxi cannery, characteristic of early-twentieth-century industrial America. Courtesy Biloxi Public Library.

Right: This May 18, 1905, Biloxi *Herald* editorial underscores city feelings toward the "Bohemians" who often spent half a year working in its seafood canneries. Courtesy Biloxi Public Library.

THURSDAY, MAY 18, 1905

FAREWELL BOHEMIANS

Far Across Potomac River They Have Gone.

But Their Return is Certain When Oysters Get Ripe.

The last of the Baltimoreans left today for the vegetable canneries of the Atlantic coast and it becomes The Herald's painful pleasure to wish them a fond farewell, as this paper is in the habit of doing each year. The Bohemian is not to be sneered at. He (or she) has peculiarities, it is true, but who has not.

Far across Potomac river,
 They have gone.
With a sandwitch of beef liver,
 They have gone.
Scoops of beer from Baltar,
Could not cause them long to falter,
Nor their plans for leaving alter,
 They have gone.

They will return next fall when oysters are ripe and it will be a pleasure to greet them once more. They add greatly to the wealth and prosperity of the places where they work and they take little away with them when they leave. Taken up one side and down the other they are good citizens. They are opposed to race suicide and may their tribe increase.

In an effort to alleviate a housing shortage Biloxi canneries, like many mining, railroad, and other manufacturing companies throughout the United States at this time built groups of small family or long row houses adjacent to their plants. Closely resembling small, paternalistic mill towns found in the southeast piedmont region, these "camps" enabled ethnic groups to live together and thus retain their cultural traits and traditions. It was not until the late twentieth century that the last of the structural reminders of these camps disappeared. During the decades prior to World War II many of the hardworking members of the ethnic groups who occupied these camps became seafood industry leaders. (*Biloxi Daily Herald*, May 18, 23, 1905, July 24, 1914; Garraty 1968)

In this 1930s image small peninsulas of shells extend from the shoreline alongside each factory. The large white expanse on the tip of Point Cadet was home to the Biloxi Grit Company. Tony Ragusin photo, National Archives.

By the late 1880s an infusion of capital from its fast growing seafood and tourism industries had transformed Biloxi into a microcosm of national urban change. Railroad-sponsored travel writers extolled the attributes of the Mississippi Gulf Coast and referred to it as the "American Riviera" and the "American Mediterranean." As early as 1875 the town had begun collecting taxes from businesses to improve and expand its streets. In 1886 with maintenance costs prohibitive, an ordinance was passed requiring all able-bodied males to work on public streets for six days each year. By 1887 the Biloxi waterfront had become so popular that the town council was forced to pass a resolution forbidding oyster houses, wharves, and bathhouses from blocking streets which ran to the water's edge. An 1877 ordinance had earlier prohibited fences from blocking waterfront access. In addition, a survey "by a competent person" of the new boundaries described in a revised 1886 town charter, including Cuevas Street on the west and Nixon Street on the east, was ordered. To accommodate local pedestrians and visitors who enjoyed strolling along the waterfront, the town council determined that "sixty feet above the high-water mark," would remain free from construction and be designated a street or public thoroughfare. Maintenance of law and order was placed in the hands of a town marshal and a secretary who were required to purchase, at their own expense, uniforms consisting of a black slouch hat, blue sack coat, vest, and trousers, all adorned with brass buttons. Intoxication while on duty was ruled a misdemeanor. (*Biloxi Daily Herald*, May 5, 1905; *New Orleans Daily Picayune*, July 6, 1896; Biloxi Minute Book 1: 1886, 1888; Cassibry 1986; Biloxi Town Charter 1875, amended 1877 and 1886)

During the last two decades of the nineteenth century Biloxi's successful seafood industry prompted the town's modernization. In the 1888 view above, fresh oyster shells used for paving surround the fountain donated by Harry T. Howard. While the town's new gas lamps appear recently polished, a loose calf can be seen wandering in the street on the left. In the 1902 image on the left, wagon traffic abounds, power and phone lines extend along both sides of Howard Avenue, and an incandescent electric light hangs above the fountain. Courtesy Scholtes Collection.

3 Birth of a Modern City

This elevated view looking north toward the Lameuse-Howard intersection, which includes the Dukate Theater rising above the business district and street cars moving in every direction, captures the spirit of the bustling, economically healthy "Seafood Capital of the World" just after the turn of the century. Courtesy of Randy Randazzo.

Birth of a Modern City

Above: Prior to the Biloxi Street Railway's installation, the Howard fountain was relocated to the foot of Lameuse Street. This 1907 image shows streetcar rails in place and overhead trolley lines joining the growing maze of utility lines. Numerous storefront signs attest to the popularity of the Howard Avenue business district. Courtesy Randy Randazzo.

Left: A new city hall and market place constructed at Main and Howard in 1895 served the city until its razing in the 1970s. In this turn-of-the-century image an apron-clad butcher stands outside the lower entrance while lady shoppers exchange greetings in the foreground beyond Hogan's grocery. Courtesy Randy Randazzo.

Lower left: In the 1920s the old city hall added a grand staircase entrance and colonnaded portico. This 1940s image shows the new entrance and a fountain which has replaced the earlier artesian fountain. Courtesy Randy Randazzo.

This unique 1912 view showing the city's quieter residential side was taken looking north along a meandering, shell-paved Main Street behind the 1895 city hall. Howard Avenue with its streetcars and business traffic lies a block to the south. Courtesy Randy Randazzo.

At the turn of the century the massive Hotel de Montross, later renamed the Riviera, occupied the northeast corner of Lameuse Street on the Central Beach waterfront. Today the site houses the Biloxi Visitors Center. The fountain in the foreground of this 1906 postcard image was moved from the Lameuse-Howard intersection during the installation of streetcar rails. Courtesy Randy Randazzo.

In the early 1890s with the development of a horse-drawn street railway, a telephone system, and an electric light plant, Biloxi began to resemble a small, truly modern municipality. Still mourning the 1889 death of Jefferson Davis, former president of the Confederacy and resident of nearby Beauvoir, Biloxi entered the new decade with a fire near its central business district that destroyed twenty-five buildings. In 1893, nonetheless, E. G. Burklin, already noted for opening a local flour mill, initiated the Biloxi Street Railway, the Biloxi Light Plant, and a telephone system. Unfortunately, September's end saw a powerful hurricane slam into the Gulf Coast, causing greater loss of life than any past or future storm with approximately two thousand dead between Grand Isle and Pascagoula. The Biloxi fishing fleet on Lake Borgne and in the Louisiana marshes was destroyed. Thirty-five Biloxi schooners were found dismasted with 105 crewmen lost. Slicing through the Mississippi Sound from the southwest, the storm wreaked havoc on all waterfront communities. In Biloxi all but three of a hundred vessels sheltered behind Deer Island sank, and all canneries on Point Cadet were destroyed. Furthermore, a large section of the Biloxi Bay railroad bridge broke apart and caused major damage, slamming against the remaining canneries on Back Bay. (Sullivan 1989; Holt 1968)

A kindly New Orleans population and the American Red Cross assured Biloxi's rapid recovery from the storm. Despite a national depression which precipitated the failure of more than five hundred banks and sixteen thousand businesses, Biloxi's seafood production reflected the booming popularity of the oyster. Lower freight rates and the shipping of containerized oyster meats preserved with artificially made ice further boosted production. Meanwhile, a population of five thousand residents allowed Mississippi Governor A. J. McLaurin to officially designate Biloxi a "city." Boasting a new city hall, Biloxi became the largest and most prosperous metropolis between New Orleans and Mobile. Its almost five dozen merchants, numerous hotels, and boarding houses enjoyed the services of two financial institutions, the Bank of Biloxi and the newly opened Peoples Bank. Its thoroughfares, free from roaming animals, sported a new electric streetcar line and sixty street lamps. Approaching the new century, its citizenry and tourists enjoyed twenty-four miles of paved streets, including Howard Avenue, which had been named in public appreciation for the many civic improvements funded by the benevolent Howard family of New Orleans. Beyond the city limits, however, cow paths and logging trails still existed, and the Pass Road remained a narrow, sandy, tree-shrouded road, dotted with occasional truck farms and pecan orchards. (*Biloxi Daily Herald,* January 31, 1896; Bilox Minute Book 2: 1896–1897; MacKenzie 1996; Garraty 1968; Holt 1968; Sullivan 1989; Scholtes 1986)

Above: Two mammoth oaks which once stood on the lawn of the historic hotel remain today. In this 1901 image guests gather on the hotel's popular "shoo-fly." A replicated "shoo-fly" around this same tree still attracts many Biloxi visitors today. Courtesy Maritime and Seafood Industry Museum.

Right: This wintry image shows east Howard Avenue. In 1900 the trolley turned south at Oak Street and ran down to the Lopez-Dukate factory. It was later extended along the Point Cadet waterfront. Courtesy Randy Randazzo.

Lower right: This image shows the western end of the Biloxi downtown business district rebuilt following the devastating fire of 1900. The T. P. Dulion Company occupied the Lopez Building on the northwest corner of Reynoir Street and Howard Avenue. The new Catholic Church of the Nativity is seen in the distance. Courtesy Randy Randazzo.

Entering the twentieth century, Biloxi boasted a population of almost seven thousand residents. A combination city map and real estate guide drawn by city engineer John Seligmann touted the city's growth and featured its amenities, including a new drainage system, sidewalks along recently paved streets, and a brick paved business district. Biloxi officials expressed great pride in the Rosell Sash and Blind Factory, the South's largest; the Chinn and Company flour mill; and the Elder and Bradford lumber yard. The seven-hundred-seat Dukate Theater, opening in 1899, a Kings Daughters library, the fire department, numerous schools and churches, and a rising boat building industry were also mentioned. Overlooked, however, was the magnificent art pottery created by the zany George Ohr, whose shop, playfully called the "Pot-Ohr-e" by the artist, was but a few steps from the center of the Howard Avenue business district. (Biloxi City Map 1900; H. Holt 1968; D. Holt 1905; Scholtes 1986)

On west Howard Avenue the scenery was that of a typical Victorian neighborhood. White picket fences and porches abounded beneath canopies of live oaks. In this period image strollers can be seen on the sidewalk in the distance next to the streetcar tracks. Courtesy Randy Randazzo.

3
Birth of a Modern City

4255 Birds Eye View of Biloxi, Miss.

The note on this elevated view of turn-of-the-century Biloxi reads "You can't see much of Biloxi here on account of the trees!" A closer look reveals oyster shell-paved streets, home gardens, arbors, and white picket fences. Courtesy Randy Randazzo.

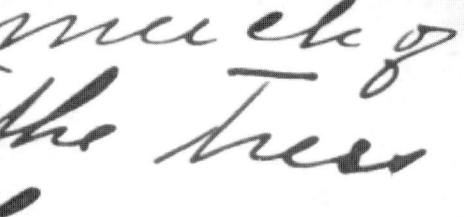

Top: This view from Delauney, now G. E. Ohr Street, looking east, shows the rich architecture of downtown Biloxi at the beginning of the twentieth century. On the left is the imposing facade of Dukate's Theater, built in 1899. Two streetcars can be seen turning the corner at Lameuse Street. Courtesy Alan Santa Cruz.

Bottom: Only a block south, on the corner of Delauney and Jackson Streets, was the fine home of Charles Redding. The home stands today, a lone survivor of several great Victorian homes once found in the heart of the city near the business district. Courtesy of Randy Randazzo.

3 Birth of a Modern City

On November 9, 1900, shortly after midnight a disastrous fire broke out in the rear of Kennedy's Saloon on Reynoir Street. By morning, shifting winds had driven the flames down Reynoir and Fayard Streets, east and west through the business district, and down to the beach. Ninety structures were lost, among them the Catholic Church, a magnificent mansion of seafood mogul Lazaro Lopez, and some of the city's best downtown businesses. Unbelievable, by the fall of 1901 most of the destroyed structures had been rebuilt, including the Louisville & Nashville Railroad Depot and the Kennedy Hotel. In mid-August during the reconstruction process Biloxi was raked by a ninety mile-per-hour hurricane. Its waterfront was severely eroded in numerous places, and a new thoroughfare, the "shell drive," was washed away. Virtually every pier and bathhouse was destroyed. Undeterred by adversity, Biloxi built a wooden toll bridge from the foot of Caillavet Street across Back Bay.

Within two years, on the eve of the oyster industry's first "Dark Age," the city's seafood industry had wrested from Baltimore the unofficial title of "Seafood Capital of the World." Its five big canneries, Lopez and Dukate, Barataria Canning Company, William Gorenflo and Company, E. C. Joullian and Company, and Biloxi Canning Company, were among the world's leading producers of processed seafood. (MacKenzie 1996; Sullivan 1989)

Above: This view looking south along Reynoir Street below Howard Avenue shows more modest Biloxi homes at the beginning of the century. Courtesy Randy Randazzo.

Right: This 1904 view shows the magnificent Victorian residence of seafood magnate Lazaro Lopez, located on the corner of Reynoir Street and Howard Avenue. It replaced an equally grand structure consumed by the devastating 1900 fire. Courtesy Scholtes Collection.

Lower right: In 1900 the palatial Queen Anne Victorian mansion and grounds of seafood magnate W. K. M. Dukate occupied a full block, facing Howard Avenue between Dulaney and Magnolia streets. Its manicured lawn was reportedly dotted with beds of rare exotic plants and shrubs. Courtesy Scholtes Collection.

For more than a century photographers have used the Biloxi lighthouse to capture elevated views of the waterfront. This turn-of-the-century view shows the effect of storm erosion on the Central Beach shoreline. Bulk-heading and shoring of properties is evident in the left foreground. Courtesy of Randy Randazzo.

Cognizant of the city's dependence on its prosperous seafood industry, Biloxi leaders sought to expand its historic tourist trade. In response to a national golfing craze, tourism-minded Biloxians built the Keller Golf Links, a fledgling nine-hole, 1,941-yard course off east Howard Avenue. In addition to a much needed amusement pavilion constructed over the water between Reynoir and Croesus streets, a fountain donated earlier to the city by the Howard family was moved from the intersection of Howard and Lameuse to the beach at the foot of Lameuse to make way for the growing Biloxi Electric Railway and Power Company streetcar line. (Holt 1968; Scholtes 1986)

Top: This early image, taken near today's I-110 loop, shows the effect of years of erosion. Visitors can be seen strolling along the tranquil shore in the distance. The large structure on the horizon is the great pavilion of the Montross Hotel. Courtesy of Scholtes Collection.

Bottom: The early Yacht Club also afforded photographers an excellent view of the Biloxi shore. In this 1904 image, piers and boat and oyster houses line the waterfront from Main Street to the canneries beyond Oak Street. Oyster shipping barrels are clustered on the wharf below the photographer's perch. Courtesy Randy Randazzo.

Taken from almost the same vantage point, this early 1960s image shows the changes that had taken place over a half century. Although factories were still active on Point Cadet in the distance, hurricanes had removed many piers. In the foreground is the old Biloxi Port Commission Office and small craft harbor. Courtesy Scholtes Collection.

With its ever-increasing amenities Biloxi became a favorite site for early conventions. In 1904 the city hosted Mississippi's annual National Guard encampment. The three regiments of civilian soldiers who attended were visited by recently elected Governor James K. Vardaman, the camp's namesake. While in Biloxi the guardsmen participated in a tribute to the Confederate veterans living at Beauvoir, marching to the grounds and sharing their rations with the aging men. After dismissing the ladies in attendance, the troops took a welcomed break and bathed on the beach. (*Biloxi Daily Herald*, June 1904; Holt 1968)

Along the East Beach waterfront moss-draped oaks shroud the shell drive leading to the factory district. In this postcard image cypress trees dot the shoreline along which visitors stroll near a "shoo-fly." Point Cadet canneries lie in the distance. Courtesy Scholtes Collection.

Above: Early postcard images of the Biloxi waterfront attracted countless visitors to the town. The idyllic scene captured in this view looking west near Kuhn Street shows why. Courtesy Alan Santa Cruz.

Right: Until felled by Hurricane Camille, the Baldwin Wood lighthouse stood on East Beach for almost a century. This early view looking west near Bellman Street shows the light tower and a magnificent wrought iron fence which bordered the shell drive in front of the property. Today the site is occupied by the Vance (Gillis) House, an antebellum structure moved during the construction of the I-110 loop. Courtesy Randy Randazzo.

Also on East Beach was the Episcopal Church of the Redeemer, as seen in this 1904 image looking beyond the famous Ring-in-the-Oak. Built in 1892 as a gift of the Howard family, the church was destroyed by Hurricane Camille. The bell tower remains today. Courtesy Scholtes Collection.

Gathered on the porch of a south Lameuse Street boarding house, these turn-of-the-century visitors appear pleased with the city's growing amenities. The fancy mill work on the porch probably came from the Brielmaier Sash and Blind Factory. Courtesy Randy Randazzo.

3

Birth of a Modern City

In 1906 Biloxi extended its corporate limits westward to the Range line near present-day Iberville Drive, thus absorbing the Seashore Camp Ground and numerous homes along the beach front. Bought out by the Gulfport-based Mississippi Coast Traction Company, forerunner of the Mississippi Power Company, the city streetcar line moved its rails westward beyond the Confederate veterans home at Beauvoir. By 1909 it was possible to travel from bay to bay on one of the most scenic trolley rides in the United States, a favorite Sunday junket of many Biloxians and visitors alike. (Biloxi Minute Book 5: 1906, Biloxi City Map 1908; *Biloxi Daily Herald*, April 9, 11, 12, 1906)

As early as 1895 citizens, including members of the Park and Civic Association, had been pressuring town leaders for additional city parks. In 1904 city commissioners finally appointed a committee to recommend suitable locations. A winter and summer Chautauqua park on a beachfront parcel between the Camp Ground and Hearts Ease Park was among the group's early suggestions. At this time Mississippi Representative Eaton Jackson Bowers of Harrison County introduced a bill in Congress requesting that the historic 377-acre Naval Reserve tract along Back Bay be given to the city of Biloxi "for park and cemetery purposes." As far back as 1818 timberlands across the central Gulf Coast had been surveyed for possible use in maintaining a wooden U.S. Navy. In November 1832 President Andrew Jackson had officially set aside several hundred acres of unclaimed public domain on Back Bay containing dense stands of magnificent oaks and yellow pine. In 1895 the Navy and the Department of the Interior had returned the tract of land to the public domain. When Representative Bower's bill passed in May, President Theodore Roosevelt awarded the land to the city. (Lang 1932; *Biloxi Daily Herald*, Feb. 26, May 4, June 13, 1906; Biloxi Minute Book 5; 1906)

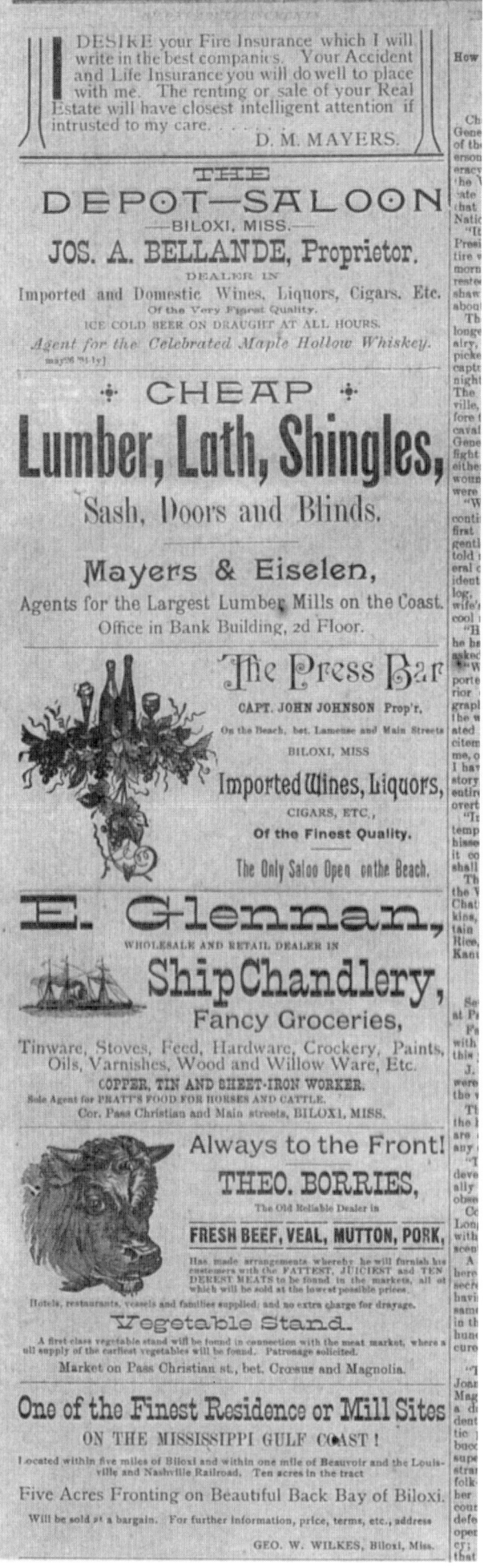

Founded in 1884 by George W. Wilkes, the *Biloxi Herald* became a daily newspaper in 1898, providing the town's merchants with a prime tool for advertising their wares. Seen here are entries from an 1895 issue. Courtesy Biloxi Public Library.

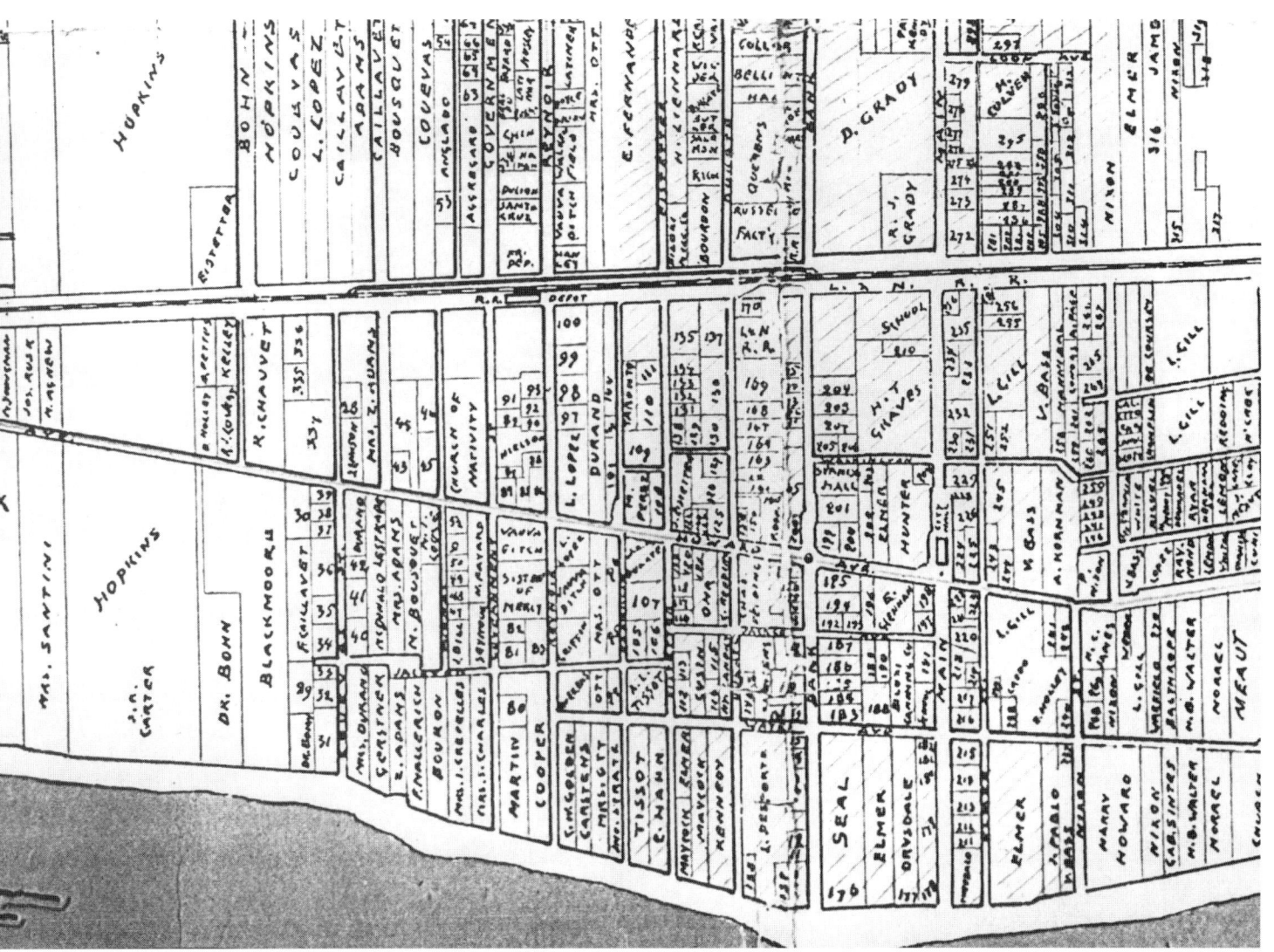

The names of property owners on this 1900 Biloxi city map afford a glimpse of the city's heritage and culture. This close-up segment shows occupants or landowners in the central business district at the turn of the century. Courtesy Biloxi Public Library.

One of the city's largest industrial complexes in 1900 was the T. J. Rosell Sash, Door, and Blind Factory located along the railroad between Lameuse and Delauney Streets. The main office of the firm appears in this image taken just after the turn of the century. Courtesy Scholtes Collection.

The interior of the main Rosell factory building was a maze of lathes, band saws, and leather belts. In this amazing view, taken inside the sky-lit main workroom, wood stock is piled high and slatted shutters of various sizes lay stacked against roof supports. Courtesy Scholtes Collection.

Sponsored by the Biloxi Businessmen's Club, a "City Beautiful" essay contest at Biloxi High School underscored the city's lack of parks, libraries, and public places of amusement. A longstanding civic need had been addressed with the securing of land in that undeveloped quarter of the peninsula. Although work on the new park began in June, a slow-moving hurricane crossing the Gulf Coast just east of Pascagoula proved a major distraction. Erosion of the shoreline at Biloxi and damage to its recently extended trolley line focused the city's attention on protecting the beach front with some form of bulkheading. (Holt 1968; Sullivan 1989)

This 1906 postcard image was taken looking north at the intersection of Howard Avenue and Lameuse Street. A horse and wagon is seen in the alley behind the Barq Building near the future site of the Saenger Theater. In the distance are hotels facing Depot Park. The T. P. Dulion store occupies the future site of the W. V. Joyce Department Store. Courtesy Mimi Stephens-Peter Webster Collection.

The Biloxi Art Pottery shop of George Ohr was located just north of the intersection of Delauney, now G. E. Ohr Street and Howard Avenue. In this 1901 image the Mad Potter poses just outside his pagoda-style complex. Courtesy Randy Randazzo.

Located in the Biloxi Library, the George Ohr Art and Cultural Center is dedicated to interpreting the life and work of the so-called "Mad Potter of Biloxi." Pictured above is the museum entrance and right, pieces of his pottery on exhibit in the museum. Courtesy George Ohr Museum.

During the late nineteenth century the L & N Railroad Depot became the entrepot for large numbers of tourists. This turn-of-the-century view of L & N Park shows the depot and hotels which once lined Reynoir Street to the east. Courtesy Randy Randazzo.

As a result of almost three decades of unprecedented seafood industry growth, the eastern third of Biloxi expanded rapidly. Streets on "the Point" were lined with the houses of boatmen, factory workers, and business owners. Small groceries, bakeries, and merchants began appearing along easternmost Howard Avenue. Although a national pure food hysteria was adversely affecting the eastern oyster market, Biloxi factories were packing and shipping more than fifteen million cases of oysters annually. However, from 1905 to 1917 the price of food nearly doubled. Stringent government shipping regulations which contributed to the increase in production costs for the oyster industry resulted in critically low incomes for seafood workers. In addition, the experienced "Bohemian" labor from Baltimore canneries, who each May with their families boarded trains to return to the Chesapeake, left Biloxi's population depleted by almost twenty-five hundred residents. Attempting to stabilize the labor force and combat the effects of a declining oyster market, local factories increased shrimp catches and began canning fruits and vegetables. In time, a number of eastern workers along with others from Louisiana opted to remain in Biloxi. (MacKenzie 1996; Durrenburger 1994; Biloxi *Daily Herald*, February 6, 1891, Sept. 2, 1895, May 23, 1905, May 14, 1906, July 25, Oct. 25, Nov. 26, 1914, Nov. 14, 1918; Thompson, *Daily Herald*, April 9, 1957)

In this late 1890s image, taken from the west side of L & N Park near Fayard Street, a number of visitors, including one on horseback, pose along the sidewalk outside the Hotel Chiapella, later renamed the Park Hotel. Courtesy Randy Randazzo.

One of the most popular gathering places for locals near the depot was Joe Bellande's Depot Saloon in the Kennedy Hotel. In this mid-1890s image several sons of Captain A. V. Bellande are pictured with mugs of the bar's well advertised cold draught beer. On the left are August and Peter, while Joe and Newt are behind the bar. Courtesy Ray Bellande.

The Pizatti Pavilion on the west side of Depot Park was constructed with tourist donations and for years served as a place for visitors to socialize. This early postcard view shows the pavilion and famous Biloxi welcome arch. The pilings for the arch still remain on the northeast corner of the site. Courtesy Randy Randazzo.

In 1908 Biloxi celebrated its first official Mardi Gras parade and dedicated a magnificent marble federal building and post office on Lameuse Street. That same year, a successful Elks Club convention held in the city convinced the Commercial Club to begin marketing Biloxi as a "convention city." By 1910 increasing numbers of automobiles in the city led the Coast Automobile Club to urge the construction of better county roads. In 1912 a coast-to-coast aviator, lured from the sky by a local businessman offering a purse of one hundred dollars, afforded many Biloxians their first aircraft view. That same year the magnificent White House Hotel opened on the waterfront at the foot of White Avenue, and the *Bernadino*, the first gasoline-powered fishing lugger on the Mississippi sound, appeared in the Biloxi channel. The ease with which it caught shrimp using a cone shaped "otter trawl," outstripping the schooner with a seine, started the wheels of change rolling in the local seafood industry. Hereafter, the weakened oyster industry began to place increasingly greater emphasis on shrimping, and the motorized vessel and its trawl tolled the death knell of Biloxi's famous "white-winged queens." (Toops 1980; Sheffield and Nicovich 1979; Holt 1968; Scholtes 1986)

Organized in the 1880s, the Biloxi Volunteer Fire Department touted their modern horse-drawn fire fighting equipment. In these 1915 views department members race down oyster shell-paved streets for the photographer. Above Mayor E. D. Glennan, sporting a white Panama hat, rides a hook and ladder unit along the beachfront drive at Main Street in front of his home. Below a shining new brass steam pumper performs for the photographer. Courtesy Scholtes Collection.

FIRE DISTRICTS.

ONE TAP—First District: Point Cadet to Howard St, south of Railroad.

TWO TAPS—Second District: Howard Street to Lameuse Street, south of Railroad.

THREE TAPS—Third District: Lameuse Street to Quave Street.

FOUR TAPS—Fourth District: Quave Street to Porter St., south of Railroad.

FIVE TAPS—Fifth District: Lameuse Street to Porter Street, north of Railroad.

SIX TAPS—Sixth District: Point Cadet to Lameuse Street, north of Railroad.

During the 1890s Biloxi was divided into six fire districts. Taps on a fire bell alerted volunteer firemen to fire locations. Cards like the one seen here defined each district and its notification code. Courtesy Biloxi Public Library.

The 1900 fire which raced down Fayard Street from the depot area destroyed the Catholic Church of the Nativity. This 1907 view shows the new church constructed in 1902, a symbol of the grand scale of postfire rebuilding in the downtown area. Courtesy Randy Randazzo.

During the years prior to the United States' entry into World War I, Biloxi continued to modernize. New businesses opened, banking expanded, and parcel post service arrived. In 1915 the new Hotel Riviera appeared at the foot of Lameuse Street on the site of the old Montross Hotel. In addition, a dance pavilion, used also for Tourist Club meetings, was constructed adjacent to a city park across from the Louisville & Nashville Depot. In June the Deer Island Amusement Park with rides, a dance hall, and vacation cottages opened on the western end of the island. Masses of mosquitoes arriving from the Louisiana marshes later in the summer contributed to the park's declining popularity. In September a hurricane's strong winds leveled large stands of timber beyond the coast. Its high tides ravaged the fledgling Deer Island park and destroyed the nearby Biloxi Yacht Club. With considerable stretches of the Biloxi shorefront eroded, trolley tracks west of the lighthouse lay undermined and twisted. Oyster schooners and other watercraft lay beached all along the shore. Tragically, seventy Biloxi schooners were caught in the open waters of the Louisiana marshes, sustaining considerable loss of lives and vessels. (*Biloxi Daily Herald*, September 1915; Sullivan 1989; Neuman and Jarvin 1987; Thompson, *Daily Herald*, April 9, 1959)

In 1900 a wooden toll bridge was constructed from the foot of Caillavet Street over Back Bay. These 1902 images feature the structure which replaced the ferry service in operation since the antebellum period. In 1927 a parallel concrete bridge was built. Courtesy Randy Randazzo.

Following the 1915 storm the seafood industry faced labor troubles. In July several hundred unionized shrimpers had presented local packers with a contract specifying wages and working conditions. In August the situation had grown more intense as packers began employing nonunion factory workers and boatmen. Owners of both schooners and seines, the packers were eventually victorious. Nevertheless, the new motorized trawler shifted boat ownership from factory to fishermen. As packers became processors, procuring shrimp from independent fishermen, the age of the large factories passed. (Durrenberger 1994; *Biloxi Daily Herald*, July 30, Aug. 7-Sept. 16, 1995)

In this 1906 image, looking west from the vicinity of Lameuse Street, a streetcar winds its way through the giant oaks near the ice wharf on Back Bay. The W. F. Gorenflo factory and the old bridge are seen in the distance. Courtesy Randy Randazzo.

Sprawling seafood canneries dotted the rim of the peninsula at the turn of the century. The Barataria Canning Company, seen in this 1913 image, occupied the eastern tip until being destroyed in the 1915 hurricane. Courtesy Joe Scholtes Collection.

Beyond the Barataria factory Point Cadet lay almost primitive. No bridge would cross the mouth of Biloxi Bay until the 1930s. In this pre–World War I image schooners enter the mouth of the bay headed for Back Bay canneries. Courtesy Alan Santa Cruz.

Early Biloxi shipyards were kept busy maintaining vessels or repairing and replacing those damaged or lost in hurricanes. Moreover, a rapidly expanding seafood industry demanded the construction of new vessels. This 1910 image shows several schooners on the ways at a Back Bay boatyard. Courtesy Randy Randazzo.

Still recovering from the 1915 hurricane, Biloxi experienced yet another, the sixth in a twenty-year period. Making landfall east of Pascagoula, its powerful northerly winds pounded factories, vessels, and shipyards along Back Bay. Those engaged in repairing the damage would have been relieved to know that the next hurricane to ravage Biloxi would not strike for another thirty-one years. (*Biloxi Daily Herald*, July 7, 11, 13, 15, 24, August 15, 1916; Sullivan 1989)

Although Biloxi boasted a modern trolley system, horse-drawn conveyances remained in use in the city for decades. This 1894 image of a horse auction near the city market on Main Street was found in the 1895 city hall cornerstone. Courtesy Biloxi Public Library.

One Biloxi business using horse-drawn wagons was N. P. Henley's Biloxi Bakery and Original Spanish Bakery located at the Main Street–Pass Christian Road intersection. In this 1895 image its delivery wagon poses in front of an oak plastered with handbills. Courtesy Biloxi Public Library.

The completion of the trolley line between Biloxi and Pass Christian provided visitors with one of the country's most delightful and colorful excursions. This 1913 image, with sightseers hanging from the cars, illustrates the popularity of Sunday outings along the Mississippi Sound. Courtesy Randy Randazzo.

Soon after its transfer to the city in 1906, the Naval Reserve became popular for picnics and excursions. In this early aerial mosaic the park and its long fishing pier are seen top center. Biloxi Stadium, Biloxi Golf Club, and Biloxi Airport are also visible. Courtesy Keesler AFB History Office.

Spurred by the lumber and shipbuilding demands of World War I, Biloxi and the Mississippi Gulf Coast experienced a brief period of rapid growth. By 1918 shipyards on Back Bay were busy constructing giant wooden hull schooners, part of a three-million-dollar, 150-vessel government shipbuilding program which centered primarily in Gulf Coast yards. The lumber needed for wooden ships and army cantonments, mostly Southern pine, created runaway expansion in local lumber production. In June the *Elizabeth Ruth*, a 193-foot behemoth built for the Australian government, was launched by the Mississippi Coast Shipbuilding Company at its yard near the foot of Oak Street. Three other large ships were also built on Back Bay. However, war's end brought a quick halt to production. Plans for expanding Biloxi's shipbuilding industry were never realized.

The popularity of Naval Reserve Park increased with the arrival of the automobile and the addition of numerous park improvements. This early twenties postcard image shows a section set aside for automobile camping. Courtesy Randy Randazzo.

One of the most popular locations in Naval Reserve Park was its central pavilion which served as a focal point for major functions. This 1920s image shows an idyllic location beneath moss-draped oaks overlooking Back Bay. Courtesy Randy Randazzo.

In this 1941 image trainees at Keesler Field are engaged in swimming classes near the park's popular fishing pier. Park benches are seen in the background. Courtesy Keesler AFB History Office.

The 1915 hurricane devastated the entire Biloxi waterfront. In this image, taken at the height of the storm, workers stand amidst debris on the eroded shell drive of East Beach. The Biloxi Yacht Club in the background was one of the storm's many victims. Courtesy Scholtes Collection.

During this period the unoccupied Naval Reserve lands along Back Bay received much attention. On the eve of World War I, the *Daily Herald* promoted its use as a military rifle range and training camp. The U.S. Army's General Leonard Wood considered it as a potential site for training high school and college graduates. In March 1916, however, the city designated forty acres of the land as a park and picnic ground for "various societies, Sunday school and other organizations" and appointed a caretaker. The site was surrounded with fences, and plans were made for adding flower beds, swings, and benches. Park supporters held dinners and even urged the sale of its timber to raise additional funds. Because of its legislated use for "park and cemetery purposes," the land was proposed as a relocation site for the small fifteen-to-twenty-grave Jewish cemetery, established in 1856 on Reynoir Street. Prior to its inclusion in the land package that would become Keesler Field in 1941, the park and adjoining property added later by the city boasted a small zoo, a major league baseball park, four softball parks, an airport, and a Boy Scout camp. Additionally, in 1925 a United States Coast Guard station was constructed on its west side at the foot of Peters Lane. (*Biloxi Daily Herald*, Jan. 12, 1916; Scholtes 1986; *Daily Herald 50th Anniversary* 1934)

Also ravaged were many of the stately homes which stood along the shore beyond the lighthouse on West Beach. The trolley rails which can be seen running along the bottom of this image were totally destroyed. Courtesy Randy Randazzo.

The Biloxi Yacht Club destroyed by the 1915 storm was one of the most prominent structures on Central Beach and the subject of numerous postcard images. This tranquil 1904 view shows the facility in calmer times with boathouses and schooners in the distance. Courtesy Randy Randazzo.

In May 1918, members of Biloxi's newly adopted commission form of government issued a charter and sold a parcel of land southeast of the park to the Biloxi Golf Club for a golf course. According to its charter, the endeavor would "advance the interests, and public welfare of the City of Biloxi and Gulf Coast of Mississippi, . . . promote and encourage tourist travel, and . . . induce tourists and visitors to spend their vacations in the City of Biloxi and on the Gulf Coast of Mississippi." Located just off the Pass Road above the White House Hotel, the eighteen-hole course which opened in 1920 hosted numerous tournaments and served Biloxians and tourists until it became part of the Keesler Field land package in 1941. Golfers were still on its fairways when workmen began clearing the land for the air base that year! (Biloxi Minute Book 11: 1918; Biloxi Golf Club Charter 1918; Biloxi Chamber of Commerce brochure 1925; *Biloxi Daily Herald,* Jan 12, Mar. 27, April 11, May 8, 1916)

Above: A new yacht club was built in 1916. In this 1922 image both the new facility and the large Montross Hotel pavilion in the background are jammed with onlookers during the annual Biloxi schooner race. Courtesy Scholtes Collection.

Right: Shortly before its destruction in Hurricane Camille, the Biloxi Yacht Club attracts a crowd to observe the annual Mayor's Cup event. Several of the yacht club's Fish Class sailboats can be seen in the background. Courtesy Scholtes Collection.

In 1905 work began on a combination post office, courthouse, and customs house. This series of images taken between 1905 and 1908 show an imposing marble structure rising from the ground on the corner of Jackson and Lameuse Streets. Courtesy Biloxi Public Library.

Above: This stark, wintry, 1940s image shows why the Biloxi Federal Building was known as one of the best Neoclassical Revival structures in the South. In the 1960s its interior was altered for use as the new Biloxi City Hall. Courtesy Alan Santa Cruz.

Left: Across Lameuse Street from the Federal Building stood the imposing Biloxi Elks Club. Built in 1912, for years it was the center of carnival balls and other social functions. It was razed in 1976 to make way for the Biloxi Library and Cultural Center. Courtesy Randy Randazzo Collection.

Although Biloxians frequently traveled to New Orleans for Mardi Gras and held their own unofficial celebrations, in 1908 an official parade was held. This 1914 image shows King E. L. Dukate and Queen Novita Lopez at the ball which climaxed their reign. Courtesy Mardi Gras Museum.

In this 1954 image, King Iberville toasts Queen Ixolib and her maids on the balcony of the historic Elks Club. Today the traditional toast is offered at the Biloxi City Hall. Courtesy Mardi Gras Museum.

When the golfing craze swept the United States during the post–World War I era, Biloxians quickly seized the moment and developed the Biloxi Golf Club off the Pass Road on land which today is the heart of Keesler AFB. In this 1940 image golfers traverse one of the fairways on the championship course. Courtesy Keesler AFB History Office.

This 1940 view from the Pass Road features the clubhouse which served golfers until the course became a part of the 1941 Keesler Field land package. The structure housed a headquarters and officers club before being razed in the 1990s. Courtesy Randy Randazzo.

During the 1920s one of the church groups which ministered to Biloxi's seafood workers was the Lutheran Evangelical and Reform Church seen here with its famous bus on the corner of Jackson and Thomas Streets. Courtesy Randall McDonnell.

The Biloxi Country Club clubhouse eventually became an officer's club and served base personnel until being razed in the 1990s. In this wintry World War II image the "officers only" sign clearly emphasizes its status. Courtesy Keesler AFB History Office.

Chapter 4

Between the Wars

During the 1920s, known as the "Dollar Decade," Biloxi benefited from the emerging automobile age. Nationally, the automobile ushered in boom conditions for a variety of industries. Billions of dollars for road construction and maintenance were spent annually. Country clubs, golf courses, roadhouses, and suburbs resulted. With tourism a national obsession, the construction of new hotels became epidemic. During the 1920s several Biloxi hotels, including the Buena Vista, Avelez, and Tivoli, opened their doors along the older, central part of the peninsula. Meanwhile, a short distance west of Beauvoir the two-million-dollar Edgewater Gulf Hotel began welcoming guests. Biloxi's 10,937 residents witnessed the replacement of horses and wagons and the electric streetcar by automobiles and a modern bus system. In 1925 a new asphalt highway, part of the Old Spanish Trail National Highway connecting San Diego to St. Augustine, began to wind its way from the Alabama line to the Pearl River. In 1926 a new thirty-four-hundred-foot concrete Back Bay Bridge, constructed at a cost of $350,000, replaced the aging wooden toll bridge which had been erected in 1901 at a cost of $1,700. By 1930 modern high-way bridges spanned all the bays and rivers on the Mississippi Gulf Coast. Additionally, a two-million-dollar bond issue was passed to build the long-awaited seawall which would provide protection for the new beachfront highway. Completed in 1928, the twenty-four-mile concrete structure was reportedly the longest of its kind in the world. (*Biloxi Daily Herald*, Jan.-Dec., 1927; Holt 1968; Sullivan and Powell 1985; *Herald Fiftieth Anniversary* 1934)

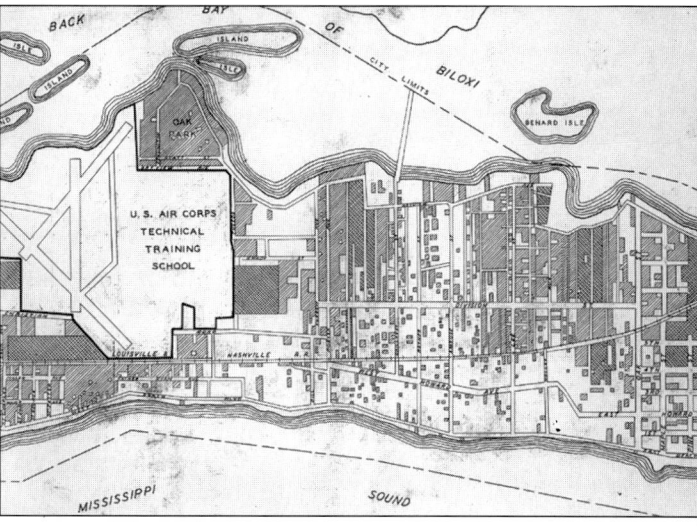

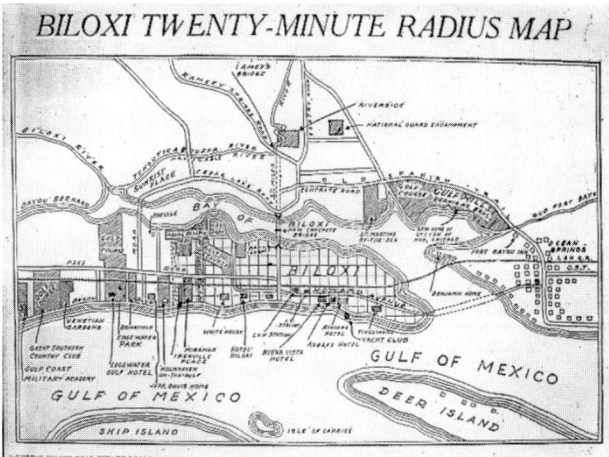

Top: This 1940 WPA map shows the extent of Biloxi's development during the decades prior to World War II. The diagonally shaded areas denote land vacant at the time of the mapping. Crosshatched areas represent land not yet developed. Courtesy Biloxi Public Library.

Bottom: Calling the Biloxi Peninsula the "Land of Great Sunshine," the Real Estate Board of Biloxi produced this 1927 map to advertise the city's numerous amenities. Particular emphasis was given to hotels, new subdivisions, and golf courses. Courtesy Biloxi Public Library.

In the 1920s a young Biloxi Chamber of Commerce initiated an advertising campaign and produced a pictorial brochure entitled *Biloxi: The Four Season Resort*. It touted the "Peninsula City's" beautiful scenery, hospitality, hotels, fishing, sightseeing, and watersports. Courtesy Biloxi Public Library.

Top: The automobile opened a new chapter in Biloxi's tourism history. In this view from the lawn of the Robinson-Maloney (Dantzler) House an early motor vehicle makes its way along the shell drive near the lighthouse. Courtesy Alan Santa Cruz Collection.

Bottom: This early postcard image shows a number of vehicles in front of the Avelez Hotel in downtown Biloxi. The hotel was constructed on the site of the early Dukate residence which today includes the Magnolia walking mall and Biloxi Regional Hospital. Courtesy Alan Santa Cruz.

Downtown Howard Avenue took on a new look as motor vehicles replaced other modes of transportation. This late-1920s postcard view looking east at Reynoir Street includes the new Kress Store which opened in 1927. Courtesy Randy Randazzo.

After Mississippi became the first state to ratify the Eighteenth Amendment in 1919, the piney woods region north of the Gulf Coast, which had been dry since 1908, became a center for the production of illegal moonshine. Numerous Biloxi fishermen participated in the illicit trade. Their knowledge of local bays, bayous, and marshes proved advantageous for those who used their boats to transport illegal liquor from ships anchored off the barrier islands through the Mississippi Sound. In 1923 Colonel J. W. Apperson, owner of the Buena Vista Hotel, constructed a resort, complete with liquor and gambling, outside of United States jurisdiction on Dog Key between Horn and Ship Islands. The Isle of Caprice's main pavilion offered casino gaming and contained a restaurant which reportedly served almost one thousand guests nightly! The venture lasted until 1931 when the methodical loss of the island's grasses and trees caused it to be reclaimed by the Sound. For decades thereafter the island's location was marked by a pipe spewing cool artesian water into the Gulf. (Scholtes 1986; Woodward 1951)

Top: Motor tourism also brought about a new wave of construction as old hotels were upgraded and new ones were built to accommodate increasing numbers of visitors. This 1940s image shows the famous Buena Vista Hotel, built 1924–1927, on the Central Beach waterfront. The Spanish-styled hotel with its stucco facade and red tile roof welcomed visitors for almost seventy years. Courtesy Alan Santa Cruz.

Bottom: During the late 1920s and 1930s the Buena Vista was the site of numerous events, including the annual Elk-Pat Fourth of July bathing beauty contest. In this 1930s image onlookers crowd the hotel's veranda as contestants parade around the entrance ellipse. Courtesy Alan Santa Cruz.

These late-1930s images feature the Edgewater Gulf, one of the grandest hotels to appear on the Mississippi Gulf Coast. Surrounded by magnificent oaks, the facility boasted such amenities as a golf course, riding stable, and its own train station. Below, a well-appointed dining room attests to the hotel's elegance. Courtesy Alan Santa Cruz.

To combat the Gulf Coast's illicit liquor trade, the United States Coast Guard installed a temporary substation on Back Bay which provided harbor service for at least one patrol boat. In 1927 Biloxi built a three-hundred-foot T-pier, warehouse, and office building on Naval Reserve land off Peters Street. Officially designated Coast Guard Base 15, the unit assisted disabled fishing vessels. At its peak in the early thirties, as many as eight 75-foot patrol boats and numerous other motor vessels operated from its wharf. Commanded by Captain S. P. Edmonds, developer of the famous Kapok lifesaving jacket, the 109-man unit boasted one of Biloxi's largest payrolls during the early Depression years. When Prohibition ended in 1933, the base was ordered abandoned. Realizing its importance to both the local economy and the safety of the fishing fleet, city leaders quickly pursued the Coast Guard and secured a new amphibious air base. Point Cadet Park on the eastern tip of the Peninsula was chosen as its site. Prior to December 1941 its aircraft conducted search and rescue missions from Appalachicola to the Mexican border. Antisubmarine patrolling was added to its mission after the United States entered World War II. (Biloxi Minute Book 13: 1927; Book 14: 1928; Book 15: 1933; Scholtes 1986; Bergeron, *Sun Herald*, Aug. 5, 1990; Pearcy 1991)

These 1922 images of the Wachenfeld and Hagan piers at the foot of Reynoir Street show a favorite pastime of Biloxi youths during the 1920s and 1930s. Courtesy Scholtes Collection.

For many years Biloxi's school system consisted of donated facilities. This 1908 image shows the splendid new H. T. Howard Primary School No. 2, located on Point Cadet. Courtesy Randy Randazzo.

Top: This 1910 image shows a variety of boating activities around Popps Ferry on Back Bay's extreme western end. The ferry was a key link to Sun Kist Farms and other truck farms on the north shore. Today a heavily trafficked causeway and bridge link the peninsula to the area. Courtesy Randy Randazzo.

Middle: The shore along Back Bay west of the wooden toll bridge lay virtually undeveloped for years. This 1912 view of the entrance to Keegan's Bayou provides a glimpse of an isolated retreat. By the early 1930s numerous subdivisions were laid out in the area beyond. Courtesy Randy Randazzo.

Bottom: In 1912 the first school funded through a city bond issue was built on east Howard Avenue. During the 1920s virtually all the old donated schools, some dating back to 1886, were replaced by new masonry facilities. This early postcard image shows Biloxi High School in the 1920s. Courtesy Randy Randazzo.

Like so many cities along the South's coasts, Biloxi participated in the resort and real estate boom of the early twenties. Since the 1870s vacationers to the seashore had arrived by rail. In the 1920s the automobile brought increasing numbers of vacationers and new residents. Prices for beachfront property soared as speculators, attracted by the city's history, ambiance, and amenities, invested heavily in local real estate. By 1926 new summer homes and subdivisions began to appear along the west Biloxi beachfront and on Back Bay. Several subdivisions were platted on Back Bay, including Bay Terrace, Lamar Beach, Biloxi Bay Addition, Oak Park, and Naval Reserve Subdivision. In addition to lots for several hundred homes, Oak Park developers proposed a park, two public beaches, and a yacht club! In west Biloxi, meanwhile, east of newly constructed Iberville Drive, surveys were being completed for Miramar Addition, Bienville Subdivision, Unger Subdivision, Coral Gardens, Pine Hurst Addition, Avondale Subdivision, and north of the railroad, Joyner Subdivision. In 1927 the openings of Edgewater and Brierfield subdivisions, then west of the city limits near the mammoth Edgewater Hotel, attracted a number of Chicagoans, including the mayor. Unfortunately, northern visitors to the Edgewater subdivision were greeted by freezing temperatures, and few lots were sold. Furthermore, the inclement weather destroyed the subdivision's considerable landscaping purchased from Avery Island nurseries in Louisiana. (*Biloxi Daily Herald*, March 28, 1927; Biloxi City Map 1930; Harrison County Supervisors Map 1927; Naval Reserve Park Subdivision Charter, 1926; City of Biloxi Tax Map 1941)

The Broadwater Beach Hotel, constructed in 1940 well beyond the city limits, offered numerous amenities to motoring tourists. This image shows the newly constructed hotel complex with some of its flanking outbuildings. Courtesy Randy Randazzo.

Top: This late 1940s aerial view of the Broadwater complex shows its unique sand beach and pier which extended four hundred feet to a pavilion over the Mississippi Sound. Courtesy Alan Santa Cruz.

Bottom: The construction of the sea wall in 1927 dramatically changed the ambiance of the Biloxi waterfront. This image shows the shoreline west of the lighthouse prior to construction. Courtesy Randy Randazzo.

In 1924 a real-estate-conscious Biloxi acquired several small parcels of land adjacent to Naval Reserve Park, including thirty-two acres of Methodist Camp Ground property near the park's entrance. By the spring of 1927 improvements in this quarter had been made, including a new water well, new water lines, and a primary entryway, Naval Reserve Road. The Biloxi Amusement Association, a group of baseball-conscious city businessmen, launched a campaign to raise twenty-five thousand dollars to develop a major league baseball stadium east of the park. Popular city commercial leagues were already playing on several ball fields, and the group hoped a stadium would attract a major league team for spring training. With the universal blessing of civic leaders, the group leased a city-owned parcel above the Biloxi Golf Club. Shortly after Babe Ruth and the New York Yankees' victory in the 1927 World Series, Biloxi Mayor John Kennedy set off to visit northern cities, hoping to attract a team for the following spring. In November it was announced that the Toledo Mud Hens, the 1927 Junior World's Champions under manager Casey Stengel, would be the stadium's first tenants! On January 30, 1928, ground was belatedly broken for the stadium, designed by well-known architect Carl Matthes. On that same day a similar ceremony was being held for a new one hundred thousand dollar Kress variety story on Howard Avenue. On March 7 after much fanfare the Mud Hens played their opener against the New Orleans Pelicans and lost. By the close of spring training Biloxians preferred reading about the expected completion of the Popps Ferry Bridge and the dedication of the new twenty-four-mile seawall.

This 1940 image along East Beach underscores the dramatic change to the waterfront by the construction of the seawall in that area. Courtesy Randy Randazzo.

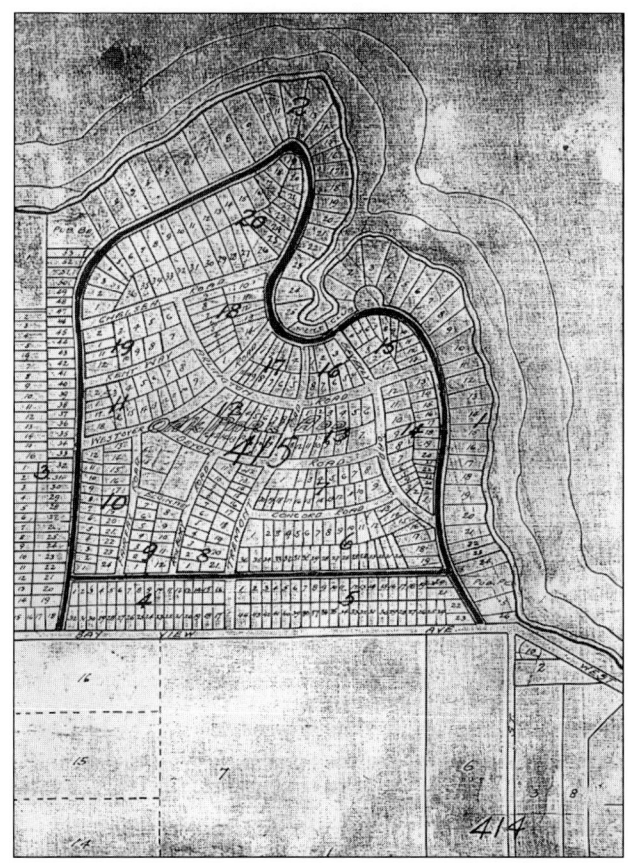

Above: Plans for the sprawling Oak Park Subdivision shown on this 1930 city map outlined a host of amenities, including parks, beaches, and a yacht club. The Depression halted development, and today Keesler housing occupies the site. Courtesy Biloxi Public Library.

Upper right: The first structure erected at the new Point Cadet Coast Guard station in 1933 was a massive steel hanger. Two of the station's amphibious aircraft, a Grumman Duck and a Grumman Goose, appear in this pre–World War II image. Survivor of numerous hurricanes, the hanger stands today. Courtesy Maritime and Seafood Industry Museum.

Middle right: This 1938 image features the main barracks at the Point Cadet Coast Guard station, a unique E-shaped building made of reinforced concrete. Used by the Mississippi National Guard after World War II, it now houses the Maritime and Seafood Industry Museum. Courtesy Randy Randazzo.

Lower right: The Popps Ferry causeway is a heavily trafficked umbilical between the peninsula and Interstate Highway 10. The importance of this beautiful land surrounding Big Lake was first noted by Bienville three hundred years ago. This 1960s aerial view looking east over the Harrison County Industrial Park shows the meandering Tchoutacabouffa River and young Sun Kist Country Club. Courtesy Hinman Collection.

This mid-1940s view of Howard Avenue looking west near Magnolia Street shows a myriad of small businesses occupying the downtown. In 1931 bus service replaced the city streetcar line. Courtesy Larry Cosper.

As the twenties drew to a close, contrary to the national trend, Biloxi did not experience the fading boom conditions. In the summer of 1928 work began on the Biloxi–Ocean Springs Bridge, and bus service between New Orleans and Mobile commenced. The Chamber of Commerce and its "Forward Biloxi" movement witnessed the groundbreaking of a new beachfront Biloxi Hospital and a Saenger Theater. In hopes of developing a local snapper fishing industry and accommodating new deep-draft fishing boats under construction at the Covacevich and other Back Bay shipyards, the Biloxi channel was deepened to ten feet. In west Biloxi, meanwhile, water service, including fire hydrants, had reached almost all of the newly platted subdivisions. As a result of pressure from the Biloxi Chamber and other civic groups, the city began planning for its own airport! When Casey Stengel returned with his Mud Hens in 1929, he noted the city's advances and proclaimed that "Biloxi . . . [is] the finest baseball camp in the United States." during the opening week of spring training that March, his team beat both the Pelicans and the Cleveland Indians! (*Biloxi Daily Herald*, Jan. 18, 30, Mar. 7, Aug. 8, Oct. 25, 1928, Feb. 22, Mar. 5, Nov. 7, 1929)

Top: After major league teams stopped using Biloxi as a site for spring training in the late 1930s, National Guard units began using Biloxi Stadium and the unfinished airport for training. In this 1938 view a Kentucky asphalt company has begun surfacing the airport's main runway while Mississippi and Alabama Guard aircraft sit near the hangar building. Courtesy Keesler AFB History Office.

Middle: This modern view shows the Saenger Theater with a restored marquee. Its first movie, *Interference*, aired January 1929. Half a century later, the city-restored-and-operated theater still serves the entertainment interests of Biloxians. Photo by the author.

Bottom: During the 1930s Back Bay shipyards continued to meet the needs of Biloxi's seafood industry. In this image taken by Tony Ragusin, several workers in the Herman Kelly shipyard pose during the framing of a lugger. From left to right they are Jules Galle, Jr., Joe Trochesset, Herman Kelly, and Jules Galle, Sr. Courtesy Scholtes Collection.

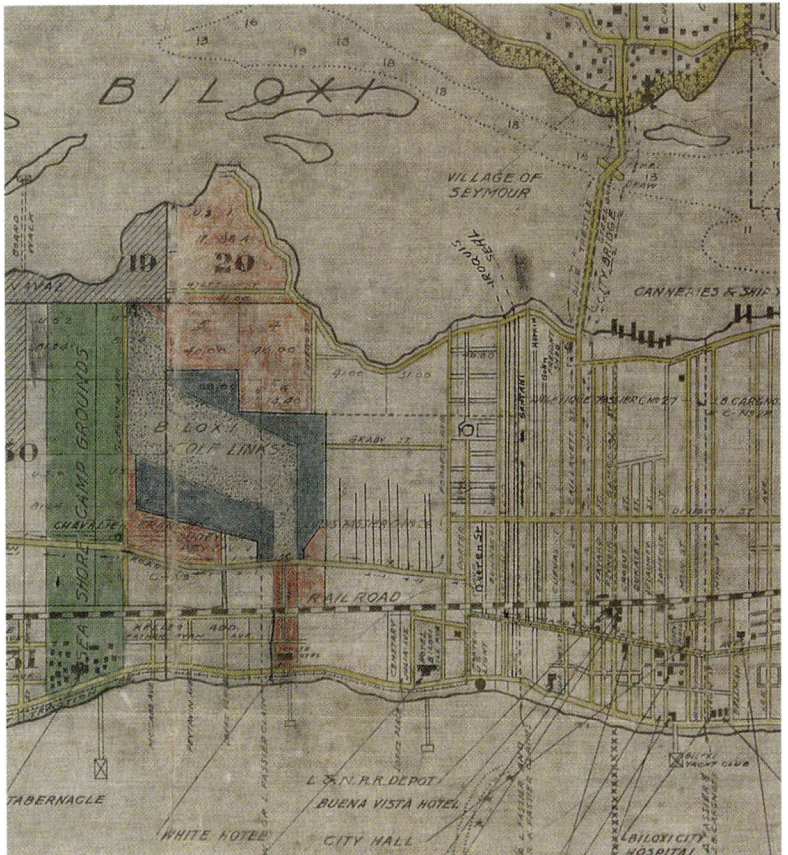

After the October 1929 Wall Street crash business in Biloxi hotels and seafood canneries continued as usual. In Biloxi, as around the nation, the effects of the Depression were not immediately experienced. The second largest seafood canning industry in the world boasted a new three-thousand-pound-per-hour shrimp cooker built by the Biloxi Machine Works. An upcoming June Confederate Veterans reunion scheduled for the beach near Miramar Park was greatly anticipated. While the Biloxi Chamber of Commerce promoted its "Beautify the Beach" campaign, its national president visited Biloxi and stressed its historic character while mentioning the narrow streets and Naval Reserve Park! Anxious to continue development in the city's western quarter, city fathers offered the state a 270-acre portion of the Naval Reserve near the Coast Guard Base for a state National Guard Camp. The city's confidence soared when the water well at Camp B. F. McClellan, the guard camp north of the coast, suddenly went dry, and units of the historic 155th Infantry Brigade and 106th Engineers temporarily moved their training to the Biloxi site. However, Biloxi's hopes were dimmed by the state's reluctance to pay for the land and its fear of abrogating the 1906 "park and cemetery use only" clause for the Naval Reserve. The water well was repaired. (*Biloxi Daily Herald*, Nov. 27, 1929, April 2, May 2, 8, 15, July 14, Aug. 29, 1930; Biloxi Minute Book 14: 1930)

Top: The 1925 Harrison County Supervisor's map shows development in West Biloxi prior to the construction of the Biloxi Airport. The city limits reach west of the Range line to a point near present-day Rodenberg Avenue. The green area represents the Methodist Seashore Assembly Campground. Courtesy Biloxi Public Library.

Bottom: In 1933 a new two-lane bridge, part of the national "Old Spanish Trail Highway," opened across the mouth of Biloxi Bay. This 1963 image shows recreational fishermen on the old bridge shortly after the opening of the present four-lane bridge. Courtesy Scholtes Collection.

Between the Wars

In this late Depression Era image the marquee on the First National Bank is advertising its 1938 Christmas Club. One of the city's new buses is making its way toward Lameuse Street. Courtesy Larry Cosper.

By 1930 the Depression had curtailed Biloxi's precipitous real estate growth. The sale of lots in many new subdivisions ceased. While some would lay undeveloped until the end of World War II, numerous parcels were claimed in lieu of taxes. As the Depression deepened, city leaders intensified promotional efforts and sought opportunities for business expansion and employment. In June 1930 the new Biloxi–Ocean Springs Bridge was dedicated during the Confederate Veterans reunion. In February 1931 a groundbreaking was held for the new veterans hospital. Claiming 640 acres of Naval Reserve land along Back Bay, the complex required additional sixty-foot-wide strips of property, paid for through a bond issue, to tie the site directly to the Pass Road and Highway 90. The project's construction kept many Biloxi workmen employed. Opening in August 1933, the "Biloxi VA" was heralded by city leaders as the greatest accomplishment in city history. In 1937 when Franklin Roosevelt arrived by train to tour the new facility, many Biloxians were given the opportunity to view an American president. The visit, which lasted ninety minutes, began at the downtown Louisville & Nashville Depot and included brief stops at the Biloxi lighthouse and the historic Fort Louis site. Afterwards he was rushed by motorcade down Highway 90 to the hospital's McDonnell Avenue entrance. Following a brief ceremony and inspection tour, the president traveled west along Highway 90 to the older Gulfport VA facility and then to a waiting train. (*Biloxi Daily Herald*, May 27, Aug. 10, 1933, April 29, 30, 1937; *Herald Fiftieth Anniversary* 1934)

Top: Begun in 1929, the Biloxi Airport project continued throughout the 1930s. In 1941 the site was included in the Keesler Field land package. In this 1941 image engineer personnel have already arrived to begin base construction. Courtesy Keesler AFB History Office.

Bottom: The development of Biloxi Golf Club, the Naval Reserve Park, Biloxi Stadium, and the Biloxi Airport necessitated the widening and paving of the Pass Road. This late-1930s view shows a narrow road running between the pecan orchards west of Naval Reserve Road. Courtesy Keesler AFB History Office.

Federal projects at the Naval Reserve Park and the Biloxi Airport provided much needed employment for Biloxians. Throughout the 1920s Naval Reserve Park had gained in popularity as a tourist destination and local gathering place. Its lengthy fishing pier, enhanced by the dumping of oyster shells and the addition of a small beach, became a favorite spot for sportsmen and bathers alike. The grounds beneath the park's moss-draped oaks were the setting for countless picnics and club functions, including the immensely popular Lions/Kiwanis Easter egg hunt which drew hundreds of Biloxi children. A small zoo opening in 1927 also attracted attention from a widespread audience. During the Depression numerous park enhancement projects funded by WPA and National Youth Administration were undertaken, including constructing cabins, planting trees and flower beds, and installing cooking grills and shelters. The park had become such a major attraction by 1940 that Biloxi Chamber of Commerce secretary Anthony Ragusin urged its promotion as the city's most important tourist enticement for the upcoming decade! (*Biloxi Daily Herald*, Jan. 15, Aug. 5, Oct. 1, 1930, April 15, 1933, June 2, July 31, Mar. 4, 1937; Biloxi Minute Book 13: 1928; Scholtes 1986)

One of the city's major projects during the Depression was the Biloxi Airport. Anxious to develop and market itself as a year-round tourist destination, Biloxi purchased a 1,398-by-4,490-foot parcel of Camp Grounds land north of the railroad. Scheduled for completion in November 1929, the project was plagued by low tax collections and the need for massive amounts of fill dirt and tree removal. In addition, increased traffic to and from the Naval Reserve Park, golf course, and stadium necessitated widening the Pass Road south of the project from thirty to sixty feet. (Biloxi Minute Book 14: 1928; Chalmers 1937; *Biloxi Daily Herald*, Nov. 20, 22, 1928, Mar. 18, Nov. 28, Dec. 5, 1929, June 3, 1930)

By 1933 the Depression had brought all city projects, including airport construction, to a virtual standstill. The city was paying its employees with borrowed funds. In sharp contrast to the six million dollars in construction contracts recorded by the city in the mid-1920s, less than $23,000 was accounted for. Like so many other financially strapped cities during the Depression, Biloxi was forced to ask the federal government for assistance. Within a year the city received funds from the Civil Works Administration, putting three hundred men to work on the airport. In the spring of 1934, however, five hundred unemployed marched through downtown Biloxi demanding jobs. By June eight Federal Emergency Relief projects, mostly paving and drainage, had provided some relief. Construction at the airport, nevertheless, was lagging. Commissioner John Swanzy was finally forced to admit that the project was more extensive than anyone in city government had anticipated. As a result, the city requested additional federal funds to move fill dirt, construct a hangar, install runway lights, add drainage, and plant grass. Low, marshy conditions in the area necessitated adding fifteen thousand cubic yards of fill to twenty thousand already hauled in! By February 1934, five years later than promised, the facility was complete enough to allow a fourteen passenger, Ford Tri-Motor aircraft to conduct fun rides. Sponsored by local Ford dealer Pringle-Reagan Motor Company and city gasoline dealers, the rides provided many Biloxians their first flight experience. (Biloxi Minute Book 15: 1934; *Biloxi Daily Herald*, May 12, June 21, July 17, Oct. 17, Nov. 12, 15, 1934, Feb. 22, Aug. 29, Dec. 31, 1936)

By late 1938, ten years after the city had begun work on the project, the Civil Aeronautics Board still had not certified the Biloxi Airport for passenger service. Although the Bureau of Air Commerce had awarded the city funds for paving the airport's three runways, building a two-story administration building and installing runway lighting, there were problems. The Veterans Administration would not allow six hundred trees to be removed from its land on the western approaches. The airport's packed, oyster shell runways, which washed out in rainy weather, were considered dangerous. Nevertheless, a few small private aircraft began landing at the field, and in the summer of 1939 aviation units of the Thirty-First "Dixie" Division used it for training. That fall, touting a "nearly" completed field, the Biloxi Chamber of Commerce unsuccessfully courted a New York aircraft manufacturer seeking a site for a two million dollar plant that would employ three thousand workers. At the same time the city was waiting anxiously to hear from Washington about a bid it had placed in the spring, with help from Mississippi Senator Pat Harrison, for a ten-million-dollar Army Air Corps training school. Unsuccessful in earlier attempts, in the spring of 1940 the Biloxi Chamber feted executives of Chicago Southern Airlines and a group of St. Louis businessmen in yet another fruitless attempt to bring air service to Biloxi. Frustrated city leaders later announced that the completion and certification of Biloxi Airport was the number one priority for the new decade. (*Biloxi Daily Herald*, Feb. 12, June 28, Aug. 7, Sept. 16, Oct. 1, 21, 24, 1937, Feb. 19, Mar. 4, Dec. 22, 1938, Jan. 9, Mar. 31, April 18, 25, May 16, June 5, July 3, 10, 11, 17, Aug. 16, 1939; Biloxi Minute Book 18: 1938)

In the spring of 1939 with an eye toward future commercial and residential development, Mayor Louis Braun launched a study of zoning regulations. On May 7, 1940, after an aggressive study which included a new city survey, public opinion, and close scrutiny of regulations used by Front Royal, Virginia, Biloxi announced its first comprehensive zoning plan. The very next day, a seventy-mile-long convoy of U.S. Army vehicles passed along the Biloxi beach front on Highway 90 headed for maneuvers in Louisiana. War was raging in both Europe and in the Asian Pacific, and the United States was preparing for any eventuality. Biloxi officials watched intently as the government initiated a variety of Defense Expansion programs. Inquiries were made into the possibility of becoming either a National Pilot Training Program site, a naval station, and/or an antiaircraft training school. Meanwhile, city leaders learned with much disappointment that as a result of a June survey by federal aviation officials, neither the airfield at Biloxi nor the one in neighboring Gulfport was suitable for commercial air traffic! The survey recommended, furthermore, that a joint Biloxi-Gulfport or Harrison County airport be built in the vicinity of Popps Ferry Bridge! On the heels of this news came word that Congress was increasing the number of military airfields and aircraft training and that the Civil Aeronautics authority was committing forty million dollars to improve two hundred fifty airports. Fittingly, the CAA maintenance office in Biloxi had only recently been moved from the Kennedy Hotel to the new Biloxi Airport hangar building, and its personnel knew well Biloxi's needs. (*Biloxi Daily Herald*, July 10, 11, Aug. 16, Oct. 20, 1939, Jan. 17, 1940; Biloxi Minute Book 19: 1939)

Above: The launching of the light cruiser *Biloxi*, CL-80, served as a major enticement for many Biloxians to join the Navy during World War II. In this image the *Biloxi*, known fondly as the Busy Bee and Double Lucky because of its many combat activities and two near disasters, cruises somewhere in the Pacific. Courtesy Maritime and Seafood Industry Museum.

Right: This classic 1930s image captures the end of the sailing age in the Biloxi fishing industry. In the foreground the schooner *Marie Foster* lies with her bowsprit removed. In the background workers load drums of fuel aboard another schooner. Courtesy Maritime and Seafood Industry Museum.

With both National Guard and Coast Guard aircraft training at Biloxi, city leaders recognized the site's future potential. Biloxi Chamber of Commerce secretary Tony Ragusin personally delivered a map of the Biloxi Airport and surrounding properties to Washington officials. Following a December 1940 visit by the commander of the Army Air Technical Training Command at Chanute Field, Illinois, Biloxi officials were notified that the city qualified as a training site. While a Biloxi delegation was at WPA headquarters in Washington attempting to secure a National Defense project in early 1941, it learned of a new training program being instituted to prepare ground service crews for fifty thousand aircraft. The delegation also discovered with delight that the Navy was going to name a new light cruiser after their city, the CL-80, USS *Biloxi*. Later nicknamed both "Busy Bee" and "Double Lucky," following extensive activity and two near fatal combat encounters, the vessel won battle honors in the Pacific and lured many Biloxians into the Navy during World War II. (*Biloxi Daily Herald*, Nov. 2, 8, 20, 1940, Jan. 29, Feb. 7, 1941; Miller 1980; Titler and Murphy 1981; Parrish and McFarland 1991)

4

Between the Wars

Top: By the 1930s many Biloxi schooners were using gasoline engines for running between the factory and reef. In this Depression Era view both schooners and motor vessels are seen. A sure sign of the converted schooner was the absence of a top mast. Courtesy Randy Randazzo Collection.

Middle: This view of the converted schooner *Mary Margaret*, built by "Jackie" Jack Covacevich and once the largest and fastest of Biloxi oyster schooners, typifies the great change brought about by the shift to motor power. Courtesy Joe Ross.

Bottom: On the eve of World War II the motor vessel had completely taken over the Biloxi fishing industry. In this period postcard view a variety of motor vessels—luggers, trawlers, and converted schooners—are docked at Point Cadet factories. Courtesy Randy Randazzo.

Top: In this mid-1950s view several wooden-hull Biloxi luggers lie at the old Kuljis oil dock. During the 1980s the area underwent considerable redevelopment and today houses a casino. Courtesy Scholtes Collection.

Middle: During the early 1960s the oyster industry profited from state conservation efforts. In this classic 1963 view by Joe Scholtes oysters appear plentiful off Pass Christian. Courtesy Scholtes Collection.

Bottom: Hand tongers also enjoyed the bountiful early 1960s. In this Joe Scholtes image, veteran fisherman Edgar Boney balances his tongs on the bow of his skiff while breaking oyster clusters apart. Courtesy Scholtes Collection.

During the Depression the seafood and tourism industries, Biloxi mainstays for almost a century, suffered greatly. The change from sail to motor power during the twenties saw the disappearance of factory-owned schooner fleets and the emergence of independent fishermen. Like farmers harvesting crops, they supplied shrimp and oysters to Biloxi factories. By the early thirties in excess of five hundred boats served the local fishing industry. For many years the fishermen received a good price for their catch. However, as the Depression deepened, seafood prices plummeted. By September 1932 low dockside shrimp prices led to unionization and a strike of twelve hundred Biloxi fishermen. A general state of unrest gripped the Biloxi industry as trucks transporting shrimp to local factories were seized and boats sunk. The following year one thousand shrimp pickers walked out when their demand for ten cents to pick twelve instead of fourteen pounds of shrimp was not met. Wages were no better for workers in the oyster industry. The best oyster shuckers at this time received an estimated fifty cents for an eleven hour day! Throughout the remainder of the decade there were disagreements over the pricing of oysters and shrimp, and packing plants often stood idle. A 1939 strike over the demand for a one dollar increase on an eight dollar a barrel of shrimp closed all Biloxi factories and kept the entire fleet in port. Similar demands in 1940 saw factories again shut down and shrimpers dumping or giving away their catches! Despite these problems the industry remained optimistic, recognizing future opportunities for marketing frozen shrimp with the new quick freeze process. In addition, Biloxi boatbuilders remained active during the period. In 1936 alone, the yards of Jules Galle, Fred Moran, Benny Yeager, U. A. Parker, "Fatty" Jack Covacevich, and Brander reportedly launched more than one hundred vessels! (Durrenburger 1994; *Daily Herald*, Aug. 29, 1936, Sept. 21–23, 1939)

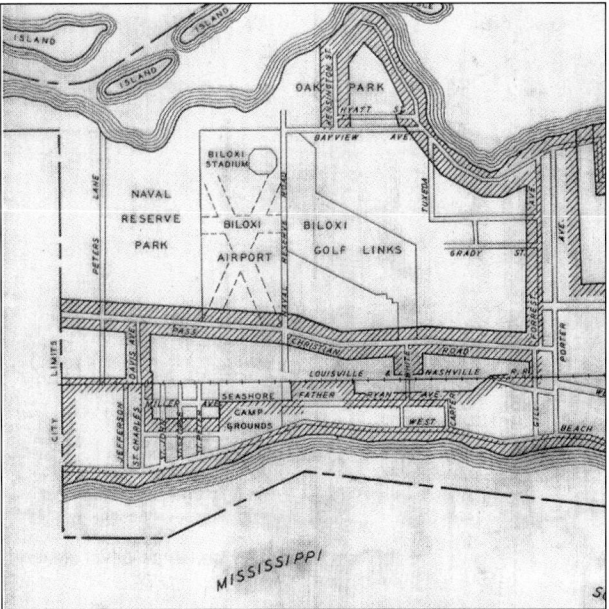

Top: Constructed on the western edge of the Naval Reserve Tract in the early 1930s, the Veterans Hospital provided many Biloxians with employment during the Depression. This late 1930s image shows the main hospital building set amidst the oaks along Back Bay. Courtesy Alan Santa Cruz.

Bottom: This 1940 WPA map shows the extent of development in west Biloxi on the eve of Keesler Field's creation. The shaded areas denote the availability of electric power. Courtesy Biloxi Public Library.

During the Depression tourism suffered nationally. The American public traveled less and resorts languished. The shortage of visitors caused a number of Biloxi hotels to close. In 1939 with travel funds cut no team came to Biloxi for spring training. Beyond that, provided by federal programs, no new city construction could be found. Optimistic about their future, however, city leaders used WPA and NYA projects to improve city infrastructure and enhance tourist attractions. Miles of streets and sidewalks were paved and parks were improved, especially Naval Reserve Park, and plans were developed to heavily landscape the median created by the four-laning of Highway 90. Much of the waterfront effort was spearheaded by the "Apostle of Beach Beautiful," Biloxi Chamber secretary Tony Ragusin. With the seafood and tourist industries struggling, the city searched for a major employer to boost the local economy. With the war in Europe and Asia filling newspapers daily and government "defense" programs on the increase, Biloxi intensified efforts to become a site for either military training or defense construction. (*Biloxi Daily Herald*, Oct. 12, 14, 24, 1938, Sept. 22, 23, 1939, Feb. 24, 1940)

Top: One of the primary areas of training at Keesler Field during World War II was aircraft maintenance. In this image an aircraft inspection class is being conducted on a B-25 in one of Keesler's large, new hangars. Courtesy Keesler AFB History Office.

Bottom: In this World War II image a camouflage class is being held under the moss-draped oaks of the former Naval Reserve Park. Courtesy Keesler AFB History Office.

The impact of Keesler Field on Biloxi's economy during World War II is readily apparent in this image which shows several thousand students in review on one of the runways. Courtesy Keesler AFB History Office.

In January 1941 Biloxi offered the Army Air Corps 832 acres of land as a site for an "air technical school." Its 164-acre airport and hangar, Biloxi Stadium, Biloxi Golf Club, Naval Reserve Park, and numerous parcels of private land not yet purchased by the city were offered. Learning of Biloxi's selection in March, city leaders scrambled to secure the required private acreage and took steps to amend the new city zoning ordinance. Since most of the package area had been designated "single family residential," a special "air technical school" zone was added. Since the deal included twenty-one hundred feet of the Pass Road, the city was left with a two-lane Highway 90 along the water's edge as the sole east-west artery. Anticipating a 300-percent population increase, the city council concentrated on expanding the city's infrastructure, proposing the construction of recreation facilities, schools, and hospitals. Although a new junior high school was built with funds from the sale of timber on the "air technical school" property, shortfalls in city revenues made it necessary to raise taxes and appeal for WPA assistance. (*Biloxi Daily Herald*, Mar. 18, 1941; Biloxi Minute Book 20: 1941; Modern Military Records Division, Record Group 18, Project Air Fields—Biloxi, No. 686; Case 1971)

On June 12, 1941, the Air Corps Station No. 8, Aviation Mechanics School in Biloxi was declared activated. Within two weeks workers under federal contract began construction on its first barracks. By early August almost five hundred workers were on site erecting the schools' 661 buildings. Estimated base construction totaled almost ten million dollars. The biggest project cost in Mississippi history, it provided for 376 two-story barracks buildings, ten mess halls, twenty-eight administration buildings, and a twelve-hundred-bed hospital! With construction underway, personnel were temporarily housed in more than 650 tents pitched in the former Naval Reserve Park, known by then as "Tent City." The Biloxi Golf Club was soon unrecognizable, covered by blocks of barracks in various stages of construction. Buildings were occupied within hours of completion! At the peak of construction more than ten thousand builders were employed, including many from the Coast. Biloxi merchants were elated! In early October the Corps of Engineers began construction of two runways, the largest almost a mile long. Although a December completion date had been projected, the discovery of quicksand, which required removal and the installation of considerable fill dirt, caused numerous delays. Both runways remained under construction until late 1942. (Biloxi Minute Book 20: 1941; *Biloxi Daily Herald*, June 5, 1941; Harrison County Deed Books, 51, 66, 150, 128, 234; Parrish and McFarland 1991; Titler and Murphy 1981)

In late June city officials suggested two names for consideration by the War Department. Proposed was Harrison Field, in honor of recently deceased Senator Pat Harrison who was instrumental in Biloxi's selection as the site for the school. A second choice was Bienville Field, in honor of Jean Baptiste Le Moyne de Bienville, governor of French Louisiana with Biloxi as capital between 1720 and 1722. In accordance with War Department policy that installations be named after servicemen killed in combat, the Biloxi school was given the name Keesler Field, in honor of Lieutenant Samuel Reeves Keesler, Jr., an aerial observer killed in Europe during World War I, whose father, a retired major general, was then mayor of Greenwood, Mississippi. (Titler and Murphy 1981)

Keesler Field added a third element to the city's economic equation. Spending by its personnel and contracts with local businesses stimulated Biloxi's growth. A lack of dependent housing on base boosted the local real estate market. Although the basic training center was shut down at war's end, troops continued to arrive, and Keesler became the largest training installation in the Army Air Forces Technical Training Command. Shortly, the focus of training was shifted from mechanics to radar and radio. In 1946-47, despite a military budget crunch which nationally reduced the number of military and civilian personnel, Keesler became the primary radar school of the Army Air Force. Locally, an increase of more than four thousand personnel was realized. In 1947 when the United States Air Force was given equal status with the Army and Navy, Keesler Field became Keesler Air Force Base. (Parrish and McFarland 1991)

During the late 1940s, both Biloxi and Keesler experienced a transitional period. While the city struggled to reestablish its seafood and tourism industries, the base strove to remain in the forefront of technical training. Many Southern communities realized major postwar industrial growth, primarily through the utilization of former war-related industries or as a result of rapidly developing petrochemical and chemical fiber industries. In addition to its governmental component, Biloxi enjoyed the fruits of its two historic income producers, especially tourism. So many visitors came south after the war that tourism in many Southern states became more profitable than agriculture. By 1954 more than four thousand motels and tourist courts had been built in the South and in Biloxi. (Ezell 1978)

Even with its limited classroom and barracks space, Keesler for years had been the home of the military's largest aircraft and engine mechanics school. Its potential of becoming the world's finest radar and communications school would never be realized without additional classroom and living space. In response to a June 1950 Communist invasion, the United States committed troops to South Korea. Soon afterwards, Keesler experienced a multimillion-dollar building program. Military call-ups raised the base's student numbers to a postwar high of 12,555. Classes began operating on a six-day schedule. The first stage of the program, which included an electronics laboratory, student housing, and dining halls, boasted a price tag of fourteen million dollars. By 1952 numerous other projects had been undertaken. New dormitories, family housing, drainage, and a major renovation of hospital facilities boosted Biloxi's economy. (Parrish and McFarland 1991)

Chapter 5

Before and After Camille

Following a thirty-one-year hiatus, on September 19, 1947, the Mississippi Gulf Coast experienced a major hurricane. After first grinding its way across Florida, the storm regained strength over the Gulf before striking the Mississippi coastline and New Orleans. Packing winds of 150 mph, the devastating right front quadrant forced a thirteen-to-fifteen-foot wall of water across the yet untested seawall. In many locations waves ate underneath the seawall and collapsed the highway beyond. In Biloxi, Gulf waters surged inland in some places for more than a block, leaving intact south of Highway 90 only the Biloxi Yacht Club and the USO building. Miraculously, a single life was lost. Coastwide, twenty lives were lost, and more than $17.5 million in damage was reported. The seafood industry on Biloxi's Point Cadet was devastated, and tourism along the waterfront, just returning to normalcy after the doldrums of World War II, was crippled. Having sustained little base damage, fifty-one hundred Keesler personnel quickly moved to the aid of the city. (Sullivan 1989)

Biloxi was a major participant in the motel craze which swept the coastal South after World War II. Numerous motels and restaurants sprang up along Highway 90. A favorite of tourists and locals alike was the Bungalow on Central Beach. Although damaged by both the 1947 hurricane and Camille, it survived until the casino era. Courtesy Alan Santa Cruz.

Top: The 1947 hurricane was the first truly damaging storm to strike Biloxi since 1915. The degree of its devastation is evident in this image taken on the Central Beach waterfront looking southeast toward the Biloxi Yacht Club. Courtesy Maritime and Seafood Industry Museum.

Bottom: Located at the foot of Dubuys Road, the Friendship House, was a coast favorite. This postcard image shows the popular eatery and lounge during its 1950s halcyon days. Courtesy Alan Santa Cruz.

The seafood industry on Point Cadet received a devastating blow in 1947. These two images show the debris near the G. B. Moore factory where shrimp boats were tossed about like toys during the storm. Courtesy Maritime and Seafood Industry Museum.

The sign of the Triple XXX Cafe is all that remains along a stretch of restaurants, motels, and gift shops which once lined Highway 90 on Central Beach. The debris from many businesses is piled high for removal. Courtesy Maritime and Seafood Industry Museum.

This aerial view shows the total destruction experienced along the Central Beach strip. In many cases the debris from destroyed structures formed a barrier which protected other buildings farther inland. Courtesy Maritime and Seafood Industry Museum.

The 1947 hurricane alerted Biloxi and the Mississippi Gulf Coast to a need for seawall maintenance and protection and strengthened shoreline building codes. Officials strongly suggested that action be taken on the Federal Beach Erosion Board's 1944 recommendation to protect the seawall by creating a sand beach. Receiving rapid approval, the project was undertaken in 1951 by the Army Corps of Engineers. South of the Biloxi lighthouse and Henderson Point, dredges began pumping six million cubic yards of sand for a three hundred-foot wide, twenty-four-mile-long beach. Completed in 1954, the longest man-made beach in the world soon became one of the Mississippi Gulf Coast's and Biloxi's most popular tourist attractions. Its popularity was enhanced by the federal government's widening of Highway 90 into four lanes. Additionally, Harrison County shoreline municipalities, including Biloxi, adopted measures placing restrictions on signage and new beachfront construction. Existing shoreline structures sustaining more than 50 percent storm damage were not rebuilt. (Meyer-Arendt 1995; *Biloxi Daily Herald*, Dec. 16, 1952)

Top: The seafood factories on Point Cadet were also rebuilt. This early-1960s panorama was taken before construction of the four-lane Biloxi–Ocean Springs Bridge. Courtesy Alan Santa Cruz.

Bottom: During the 1950s and 1960s the Central Beach strip reemerged along a new, four-lane Highway 90. This image, taken from the new Buena Vista Hotel crosswalk, illustrates the strip's revival. Popular Baricev's Restaurant appears in the distance. Courtesy Alan Santa Cruz.

The central business district on Howard Avenue was little changed from the 1930s. This view looking east from Fayard Street shows the downtown area. Courtesy Alan Santa Cruz.

Top: One of the most popular family tourist attractions during the 1960s was a cruise aboard the *Sailfish*, seen here leaving the Biloxi small craft harbor with Captain William Gorenflo at the helm. Courtesy Scholtes Collection.

Bottom: Many visitors enjoyed a fishing trip aboard one of the charter boats berthed at the Small Craft Harbor. In this early 1960s image Ralph Baker, captain of the *Sea Queen*, poses with a recently returned party of happy fishermen. Courtesy Joe Scholtes Collection.

The widening of Highway 90 along the Biloxi beachfront was part of a World War II–spawned program to lace the country with military superhighways. In Biloxi the program stimulated the growth of tourist-oriented businesses, principally restaurants and motels. Increased numbers of travelers were brought into direct contact with the city's waterfront amenities. Another wartime government project which benefited the Biloxi area was the construction of a protected Intracoastal Waterway between Florida and Texas, designed to move military materials without U-boat interference. Improved perpendicular channels linking it to coast cities provided the impetus for long-needed industrial development. Locally, the Harrison County Seaway evolved. Created in 1956, the Harrison County Development Commission used funds from an historic, oft-amended, prewar gasoline tax to develop several industrial parks along the waterway. On the eastern tip of the Biloxi Peninsula an eighty-three-acre site called Rhodes Point became the home of several light marine industries. (Meyer-Arendt 1995)

An early arrival along the "West Biloxi Strip" was Gemmill's Bar-B-Q King drive-in restaurant located on the site of today's Emerald Beach Motel. Fill being used to build up low areas south of the highway is seen in the background. Courtesy Ed Gemmill.

The combination of sand beach and superhighway led to the development of the "West Beach Strip," a six-thousand-foot-long recreational business district just beyond Biloxi's western city limits. The early beach highway had been forced to skirt the once low and marshy area. Where the seawall was buried by the sand beach, a strip of land was created and claimed by developers for numerous small structures. During the 1960s business complexes jutting into the Sound were constructed, including the Broadwater Marina which proved beneficial to both private boat owners and the rapidly expanding charter boat industry, previously limited to dockage on the central beach. Similar developments occurred along the central Biloxi waterfront. Years of shell depositing by oyster houses and the creation of a sand beach during the Depression had already witnessed extensive commercial development south of the highway. Hurricane damage along its western edge in 1947 and widening of the highway in the early 1950s prompted the construction of a secondary seawall about 250 feet south of the old wall. Subsequent backfilling created even more useable acreage and allowed the further expansion of tourist businesses south of the highway. (Meyer-Arendt 1995)

Middle: During the 1940s and 1950s the historic Robinson-Maloney House north of the lighthouse was Notre Dame High School for Boys. A new school, today called Mercy Cross, opened in 1959 along Keegan's Bayou. Courtesy Larry Cosper.

Bottom: Keesler AFB expanded rapidly during the immediate post–World War II years. This late-1940s image shows several of its many classroom buildings. The fuselage of an aircraft appears in the background. Courtesy Keesler AFB History Office.

Top: This early-1960s view features Back Bay and the eastern portion of the Biloxi Peninsula. The new four-lane bridge across the mouth of the bay is seen in the distance. Courtesy Joe Scholtes Collection.

Bottom: A popular, postwar gathering place was the Biloxi Community House on Central Beach. In this 1930s image workmen are busy completing its west wing. Heavily damaged by Camille, the building was razed. Mounted cannon barrels seen in the foreground still remain. Courtesy Randy Randazzo.

During the early post–World War II period, the Biloxi seafood industry underwent major change. A worldwide demand for protein sources caused international seafood production to quadruple as national fishing fleets expanded and increasingly sophisticated fishing technology evolved. Second only to Japan in 1948, the United States was slow to respond to the increased demand for seafood. Within two decades it had dropped to sixth in world production! For many years shrimp had been a Biloxi mainstay. Before 1930 the Biloxi industry had been supported primarily by catches of white shrimp in near-shore waters. As early as 1939 Biloxi shrimpers were harvesting significant catches of brown shrimp off the mouth of the Mississippi at forty-fathom depths. However, the first commercially important catches, made off the coast of Texas, were not reported until 1947. When exploratory shrimp fishing by the U.S. Fish and Wildlife Service in 1950 confirmed shrimping grounds east and west of the Mississippi Delta, the Mississippi Gulf Coast industry began to revive. As the demand for Gulf shrimp increased, the single-rigged Biloxi lugger, backbone of local fleets since the early 1930s, found itself competing with large, double-rigged trawlers which shrimped year round, easily working the deep water, brown shrimp sanctuaries. Accustomed to harvesting both oysters and shrimp, the Biloxi lugger found change difficult. Although newer rigs and electronic equipment were added to some shrimpers and a few trawlers joined its fishing fleet, Biloxi's percentage of total Gulf landings decreased. (Lyles 1974; Osborn, Meghan, and Drummond 1963)

Top: In the 1950s the annual Blessing of the Fleet ceremony was moved to the channel near the Biloxi Yacht Club. In this 1960s image the *Captain Blood* is passing the blessing boat. In the background crowds jam the piers behind the U.S.O. building, today the site of the Port Commission building and Glennan Park. Courtesy Hinman Collection.

Bottom: The Blessing of the Fleet, a popular annual event, began in 1929. This image shows Father F. H. Hilderbrand standing between the oyster car rails at a Point Cadet factory as he blesses each vessel. The altar boy standing on the plank is Wilmont Boudreaux. Holding the cross is Yankie Barhanovich and Edmond Boudreaux is on the right. Courtesy Boudreaux family.

Top: Typical of the boats which paraded in the 1960s blessings was the *Cajun*, a classic wooden-hull Biloxi lugger. Courtesy Scholtes Collection.

Middle: In this image passengers move toward the bow of the *Pacific* to receive the blessing as she maneuvers past the blessing boat, the *Joan Fayard* near the Biloxi small craft harbor. Courtesy Scholtes Collection.

Bottom: The selection of the Shrimp Queen has long been a highlight of the Shrimp Festival. In this 1983 image, King Tommy Schultz views the contestants. Courtesy Blessing Committee.

Right: The *Lady Sonya*, winner of the best decorated in its class, leads the 1983 Blessing of the Fleet boat parade down the Biloxi channel. This historic annual event is still one of the city's major tourist attractions. Courtesy Blessing Committee.

The Biloxi oyster industry which had reigned supreme from 1880 to 1940 also experienced significant change. During the 1940s poor management practices and unfavorable weather conditions plunged harvests from native reefs into a sharp decline that lasted almost two decades. During the post–World War II period, the rapid growth of communities and their industries along many rivers and estuaries throughout the country was repeated along the Mississippi Gulf Coast. The subsequent discharge of polluting effluents contributed to the overall decline in local oyster production. As early as 1945 highly productive reefs on Back Bay were closed. When reefs extending to Deer Island were shut down, the loss to local industry was estimated at one million dollars. In 1960 Mississippi responded to the need for better management of its oyster bottoms by creating a state Marine Conservation Commission. Between 1960 and 1969 following the regulation of oyster harvesting, a shell planting program, and the transferal of oysters from polluted to clean waters, local production quadrupled. (Lyles 1974; MacKenzie 1996)

In 1953 the National Weather Service began giving feminine names to hurricanes. On September 24, 1956, Biloxi had its first brush with a female storm. A weak Hurricane Flossy emerged from the Gulf, crossing the mouth of the Mississippi and sweeping through Biloxi on its way to the Florida Panhandle. In 1960 Hurricane Ethel, packing 150 mph winds, slammed into a cold front and fell apart just short of landfall between Biloxi and Pascagoula. In 1965 Hurricane Betsy blasted the city, its first in almost two decades. Aided by new satellite photography and information from hurricane seeking aircraft, the recently appointed Civil Defense team of Wade and Julia Guice guided the coast population in its storm preparedness. On September 9 the Mississippi Gulf Coast was ravaged by winds gusting to 100 mph and tides ranging from ten to fifteen feet. As in 1947 commercial buildings along Biloxi's central beach and the western "Strip" sustained heavy damage. Although Biloxi beaches were piled high with debris, the area suffered far less than Louisiana, where tens of thousands were displaced and dozens of lives lost. In Betsy's wake Harrison County supervisors enacted measures to prevent illegal structures from being built along the beach. The wisdom of their efforts bore fruit four years later. (Sullivan 1989)

Top: The opening of Edgewater Mall in 1967 propelled Biloxi into the modern age of merchandising. This aerial view shows the new mall along with the venerable Edgewater Gulf Hotel. Courtesy Alan Santa Cruz.

Middle: This 1964 image was taken from the west end of Deer Island during the annual Outboard Jubilee. It captures the entire Central Biloxi waterfront from the Buena Vista to the U.S.O. building. Courtesy Scholtes Collection.

Bottom: In 1956 Keesler Air Force Base personnel staged a massive off-base parade down Highway 90 to emphasize the annual Armed Forces Day theme of "Power for Peace." In this image taken from the top of the Biloxi lighthouse students move east along the highway. The sparkling new sand beach lies before the old seawall. Courtesy Keesler AFB History Office.

Top: This 1950 view of the Biloxi Mardi Gras parade looking down from above Grant's Drugstore on the corner of Reynoir and Howard shows the Barqs Bottling Company's entry, complete with musicians. Courtesy Gulf Coast Carnival Association.

Bottom: This view of the 1953 Mardi Gras parade, looking east along Howard Avenue from the Barq Building, captures the essence of post–World War II Biloxi. In the foreground is the famous Sacred Heart High School all-girl band. Courtesy Gulf Coast Carnival Association.

Top: The 1962 Biloxi Mardi Gras parade witnessed record crowds jamming the Howard Avenue parade route. In this image Matt Lyons attempts to direct a float through an almost solid wall of revelers. Courtesy Gulf Coast Carnival Association.

Bottom: With Christmas decorations strung between power poles at the intersection of Main and Howard, the Biloxi High School Indian Band parades past the old Biloxi City Hall in this mid-1960s image. Courtesy Scholtes Collection.

In the early 1960s the Cold War held center stage. In 1961 the Berlin Wall was erected, followed by the failed Bay of Pigs invasion. In 1962 the nation's attention was focused on the Cuban Missile Crisis, and in 1965 President Lyndon Johnson increased United States forces in Southeast Asia. Growing manpower demands and the need for adapted space-age and television technologies precipitated the construction of modern facilities at Keesler and the revision of its technical programs. Part of the Military Assistance Program, non-jet pilot training reported the training of 743 South Vietnamese pilots. In 1968 on the eve of Hurricane Camille, Keesler boasted fourteen thousand students and one million graduates! (Parrish and MacFarland 1991)

Top: This late-1960s aerial view looking northwest over the heart of old Biloxi shows the city just before it was hit by Hurricane Camille. The storm surge which struck this Central Beach area ranged as high as eighteen feet. Courtesy Hinman Collection.

Bottom: The new Biloxi Regional Hospital off Lafayette Street, seen in this 1960s image, served Biloxians until a new facility was constructed in the heart of the old downtown along Reynoir and Jackson Streets. Courtesy Scholtes Collection.

These two early morning 1960s views, top, looking north along Lameuse Street toward Klein's Bakery and bottom, looking south past the old Buck Theater and Question Mark Lounge toward the Sound, carry an anticipatory air. Courtesy Scholtes Collection.

On the eve of Camille the West Biloxi Strip was anchored by the revamped Broadwater Hotel complex with its new canopied marina. These images show the new facility and a large segment of newly annexed west Biloxi. Courtesy Steve Hankins.

The scene between Lameuse and Main Streets following Camille's landfall was one of total destruction. The Biloxi Yacht Club once stood on the pilings in the foreground. Courtesy Hinman Collection.

A block to the west between Lameuse and Magnolia Streets virtually nothing remained south of Highway 90. Located in this area were the Harbor Light Restaurant, Biloxi Roller Rink, Pastime Cafe, and the Pattison Pontiac Showroom. Courtesy Hinman Collection.

Since August 18, 1969, Biloxi's history has often been referred to in terms of "B. C.," before Camille, or "A. C.," after Camille. So devastating was this hurricane to Biloxi and the central Mississippi Gulf Coast, that it was as if one life had ended and another begun. Its infancy spent off the West African Coast, Hurricane Camille matured in the Caribbean and hammered western Cuba. Gaining strength on a northerly course across the Gulf, the hurricane was tracked by aircraft that recorded a barometric pressure of 26.6, the lowest ever, and winds in excess of two hundred mph. As the mighty hurricane slammed ashore, wind gauges broke with gusts of at least 230 mph. Near Pass Christian, at the hurricane's center, a storm surge of twenty-five feet was recorded. At Biloxi, a storm surge of twenty feet was reported along with eighty tornadoes. Fortunately, many coastians had taken seriously the urgent warnings of Wade Guice and evacuated the shoreline. Others not leaving paid for the mistake with their lives. Hurricane Camille left sixty-eight square miles of total destruction, more than that of the atomic bomb at Hiroshima. (*New Orleans Times-Picayune*, Aug. 22, 1969; Sullivan 1989)

On Point Cadet a fifteen-to-seventeen-foot-high storm surge washed over the peninsula. Many homes were totally destroyed. Factories, evident from this before and after image, were completely demolished. Courtesy Hinman Collection.

The destruction was just as complete between Magnolia and Fayard Streets where the Bungelow Restaurant and Motel, two service stations, Souvenir City, John Gimma Plymouth, and the Trailways Bus Station once stood. Courtesy Hinman Collection.

On the western edge of the Central Beach waterfront the Buena Vista Motel lay gutted. One door east lay what was left of Baricev's Seafood Harbor. Courtesy Hinman Collection.

Above: Near the Fiesta and Sun'n Sand motels on the West Biloxi Strip the storm surge reached beyond nineteen feet and the destruction was as complete as on Central Beach. In this view massive amounts of debris can be seen north of the highway. Courtesy Hinman Collection.

Right: Historic *Beauvoir*, survivor of more than a century of hurricanes, looked as if it had been caught in a swirling battle. Its unique raised construction allowed some of the nineteen-foot wall of water which struck this portion of the coast to pass beneath it and it survived again. Courtesy Hinman Collection.

A Force Five hurricane on the Saffir-Simpson scale, the most powerful ever to strike the continental United States, Camille battered a Biloxi poised to fulfill its historic potential. So severe was the storm's devastation that the city's future as well as its past lay in waste. In Biloxi alone, more than eleven thousand homes and sixty-five small businesses were damaged or destroyed. Fifteen deaths were recorded. Property losses were put at hundreds of millions of dollars. The seafood industry on the Biloxi Peninsula, especially on historic Point Cadet, lay in ruin. Where the hurricane surged across the peninsula, scattered cans were all that remained of some processing plants. Along the waterfront, restaurants and motels, the backbone of local tourism, were destroyed. Numerous historic structures which had graced the Biloxi Peninsula, surviving countless storms since antebellum times, were battered or demolished. The stories of survival and human caring recounted in Camille's wake, however, gave evidence to Biloxi's true historic character and will to survive. (Seafood Industry Museum, Camille file; Sullivan 1989)

Hurricane Camille left Biloxi and the entire Mississippi Gulf Coast to face nightmarish realities. Utilities and communications were out; roads were impassable; bridges were destroyed; and food, water, and fuel were in limited supply. Enormous, tangled masses of debris, often several blocks inland, extended from Biloxi to Henderson Point. Whole or in part, boats, piers, oil tanks, barges, vehicles, and homes were strewn the length of historic Highway 90 from Biloxi to Bay St. Louis. The new four-lane Biloxi–Ocean Springs Bridge, although intact, had huge sections knocked out of alignment. Remarkably, the sand beach and the seawall withstood the forces of Camille relatively well. Enveloped by the enormous storm surge, both reappeared covered with flotsam when the water receded. (MSIM Camille file; *The Daily Herald Centennial Edition*, Oct. 7, 1984)

As the powerful remnant of Hurricane Camille moved northeast through Kentucky, West Virginia, and Virginia, wreaking havoc and destruction in the Appalachians, Biloxi began the most awesome recovery task in its history. Biloxians witnessed the greatest single disaster relief effort in United States history. Keesler personnel, Navy Seabees, Mississippi National Guardsmen, and countless volunteers and federal agencies converged to help in the recovery. Impressed by the magnitude of the hurricane's destruction, President Richard Nixon became the first president to visit the Mississippi Gulf Coast since Roosevelt's tour in 1937. The president's arrival at the Biloxi-Gulfport Regional Airport in the storm's aftermath stirred the survivors with renewed hope for the future. A variety of low-interest government loan programs provided the stimulus for individual and small business recovery and for the restoration of the almost totally decimated seafood industry. (Sullivan 1989)

In the aftermath of Hurricane Camille, Biloxi residents began slowly to rebuild. For decades numerous beachfront lots were left vacant, their sets of concrete "steps to nowhere" bearing mute testimony to the devastation. Stringent building codes retarded, but did not prevent the rebuilding of businesses along Biloxi's glittery beachfront strips. Between 1972 and 1973 a two million dollar sand beach replenishment program, previously scheduled for 1969, restored that tourist attraction to its former splendor. Spurred by Biloxi's hurricane notoriety, the Air Force transferred its Fifty-Third Weather Reconnaissance Squadron from Ramey Air Force Base in Puerto Rico to Keesler. The squadron's C-130 "hurricane tracking" aircraft soon became a welcomed sight in the skies over the Mississippi Gulf Coast. Regardless of Biloxi's return to normalcy, Camille's specter haunted the tourism industry. The worldwide "energy crisis," which affected almost every facet of American life during much of the 1970s, only contributed to the crisis. (Parrish and MacFarland 1991)

Developed in the late 1970s, the Mississippi Coast Coliseum and Convention Center has played an integral role in Biloxi's post-Camille reemergence. This 1998 image shows the newly expanded complex. Courtesy Tommy Triplett and Buford Myrick.

Aided by low-interest government loan programs, Biloxi's seafood industry made a rapid recovery. However, newer vessels and processing methods which began to appear after Camille were accompanied by higher operating costs and increased competition. Improvements in refrigeration technology and transportation, both highway and marine, further reduced the need for the old dockside factory. As a result, the Biloxi seafood industry, having missed the proverbial "boat," experienced an economic crisis. Consequently, some of the older seafood businesses converted to warehouses for frozen storage and distribution. Fuel dock and staging areas for fishermen were also popular alternatives. In addition, new cold-storage facilities serviced by refrigerated motor-carrier developed off the beach. (Lyles 1974)

In this early-1980s view Vietnamese fishing boats with their "chop-stick" rigs lie near a factory on Point Cadet. Courtesy Tom Rankin.

In 1965 Biloxi virtually doubled its size and population by extending its western city limit to Debuys Road. Absorbing those neighborhoods which had developed in that quarter since the 1920s, the city also acquired the fabled "West Biloxi Strip" and Edgewater Mall, the Mississippi Gulf Coast's entry into the world of modern suburban merchandising. In the early 1970s following the demolition of the adjacent Edgewater Gulf Hotel, the Mall added forty stores. Spurred by a general population move away from the historic, century-old central business district, city leaders embarked on a program of downtown revitalization. Like many older communities throughout the nation facing a similar phenomenon, Biloxi used federal Urban Renewal funds to create a pedestrian walking mall. A four-block section of Howard Avenue, containing some of the city's most historic architecture, was canopied and renamed the *Vieux Marche'* or Old Market. Parking was added to the mall's periphery. An award-winning, multimillion-dollar library and cultural complex was constructed, and the historic Saenger Theater, which had burned in 1974, was refurbished. Failing to duplicate weather conditions and acquire an attractive commercial mix, however, the Vieux Marche' was unable to achieve the Edgewater Mall's success. As the suburbs grew, the downtown area declined. In 1977 the city attempted to offset the economic recession by expanding its tax base. The suburban area north of the western terminus of Back Bay was annexed. The Mississippi Coast Coliseum and Convention Center which opened the same year was also predicted to infuse new life into tourism with its concert and convention business. The historic Pass Road was widened to provide a new commercial corridor, and a recently opened Interstate 10 made the Mississippi Gulf Coast more easily accessible. In addition, this vital highway link allowed Biloxi planners to target areas far beyond the historic Deep South when preparing for future decades. (Biloxi Comprehensive Plan 1979; Vogt 1980; Biloxi Market Analysis 1994; Benbow 1984)

During the late 1970s the nation was in the throes of austerity from post-Vietnam streamlining. Keesler responded to a General Accounting Office suggestion to reduce military training costs by adjusting its training regimen. As a result, student numbers at Keesler dropped below five thousand for the first time since the late 1940s. The downward slide, however, was only temporary. In the early 1980s the Shah of Iran's ouster and the taking of American hostages in Teheran coupled with a Soviet missile threat renewed congressional interest in a strong military. As a result, Keesler received an increase in both training funds and students. Training in the airborne warning and control system (AWACS) and the ground-launched cruise missile was stepped up. In 1981 a strike by the Professional Air Traffic Controllers Organization and President Reagan's subsequent firing of striking controllers led to an expanded air traffic control program. In the early 1980s Keesler's overall annual economic impact on Biloxi and the Mississippi Gulf Coast was estimated at $425 million. (Biloxi General Market Analysis 1984)

Chapter 6

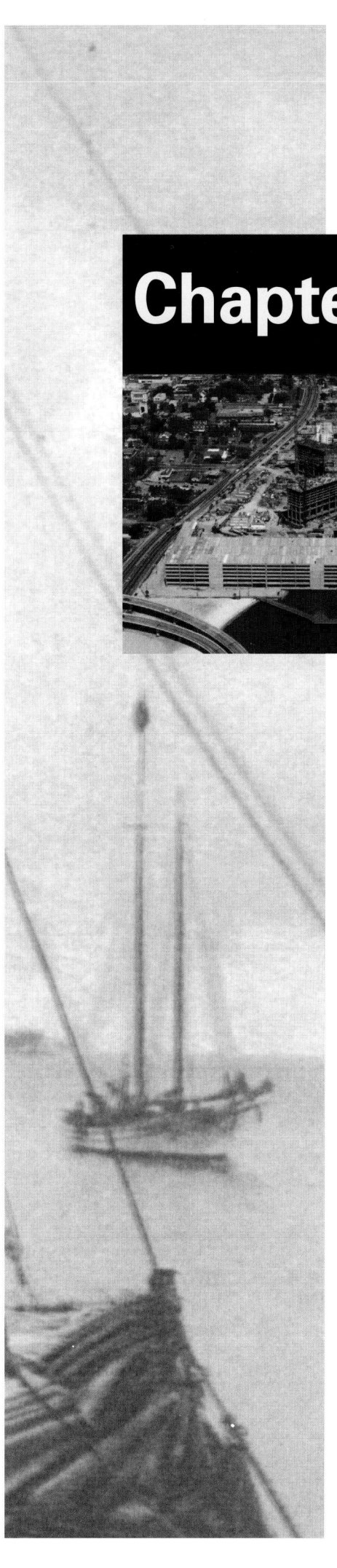

Tracing its roots to the early eighteenth century, Biloxi's Black population has long played an essential role in the town's economic development and is a key ingredient in its ethnic gumbo. During the years prior to mechanization, Blacks stood alongside White factory workers at the picking tables of Biloxi's labor intensive seafood industry. Many Black families operated their own fishing boats. During the late 1950s and early 1960s, African Americans actively sought redress from unfair laws which for years had prohibited and denied them full citizenship. On both local and national levels monumental efforts by valiant Black leaders resulted in court cases which gave everyone access to public facilities and education guaranteed by their constitutional and civil rights. Dr. Gilbert R. Mason, local NAACP president, led the effort in Biloxi.

Since the late nineteenth century, the nucleus of Biloxi's African American professionals, businesses, and civic and social enterprises was centered along present-day Main Street. In 1886 general education for Black youths began with the opening of Biloxi Colored School which later became Nichols. In 1917 Our Mother of Sorrows opened for Black Catholic children. In 1977 the Catholic Diocese of Biloxi became the first in the United States to have a Black Bishop, the Most Reverend Joseph Lawson Howze, as Ordinary. Today the Black community continues to be an integral element in Biloxi's ethnic mix.

Following the April 1975 fall of South Vietnam, refugees familiar with coastal fishing and seafood processing began arriving on the Mississippi Gulf Coast. Within a short time, these primarily Catholic Vietnamese families had repeated the amazing socioeconomic phenomenon of the decades past when Dalmatians and Cajuns meshed with the Biloxi fishing community. Arriving during a national economic recession, many were compelled to eke out a living as oyster shuckers and shrimpers within a sluggish seafood industry. While some built their own Vietnamese-style fishing vessels with peculiar "push-pole" or "chop-stick" rigs, others refurbished older Biloxi boats. Within a decade, newer steel-hull trawlers had become an integral part of the local fishing fleet. Biloxi's already rich ethnic gumbo was spiced with a Vietnamese flavor.

Toward a New Millennium

In September 1979 Hurricane Frederic's near miss left Biloxi's population of fifty thousand somewhat edgy. Although numerous vessels lay submerged in Back Bay, the storm's worst damage had actually occurred in Mobile. As the new decade opened, Keesler was the city's largest employer, supporting more than thirty thousand persons with close to a $500 million payroll. In total, government employment accounted for more than one-fifth of all available jobs in Biloxi. (Landry et al. 1985)

In the 1980s Biloxi's century-old seafood industry experienced a major transition. Although the once great fishing fleet of Biloxi's pre–World War II halcyon era was but a shadow of its former self, the sluggish $175 million industry still provided twenty-five hundred jobs. Processing plants were the major employers, while ancillary services, such as boat building and repair, marine supply, and sport fishing, accounted for many others. With the emergence of new technologies, however, many fishermen abandoned the water. Smaller catches and high fuel prices contributed to the woes of an already dwindling fishing fleet. With only one processor still canning shrimp, and another, one of Biloxi's largest, pet food, the seafood industry experienced further difficulties. Residential and commercial growth along once-virgin bays and bayous eliminated the natural breeding grounds of shrimp. Unusually heavy, local spring rains and flooding within the Mississippi River Basin, especially in 1983, caused the opening of emergency spillways in Louisiana. The resulting reduction in water salinity upset growth cycles and significantly reduced shrimp harvests. Oyster landings were also unpredictable. Despite a resurgence of the shell fish's popularity during the early 1960s, the combined impact of Hurricanes Betsy and Camille along with inadequate sewage treatment rendered many reefs unsafe for harvesting. Annual production during the 1970s averaged one third less. During the 1980s improved municipal sewage systems significantly reduced bacterial counts, and oyster landings increased. However, estimates of the time necessary to recover former highly productive reefs ranged as high as fifty years! Cold storage processing of shrimp and wholesaling and retailing operations offered the seafood industry its best hope for future success. (MacKenzie et al. 1997; Lyles 1976; Eleuterius 1976)

Top: The relocation of the historic Brielmaier and Foretich houses and the replication of a "shoo-fly" between Main and Lameuse Streets to create a Biloxi Visitors Center exemplify the city's renewed spirit and emphasis on its history and heritage. Courtesy Maritime and Seafood Industry Museum.

Bottom: One of the oldest buildings in Biloxi and one of its few remaining structures from the antebellum period, the "Old Brick House" has been preserved by the City and is the scene of numerous annual events. Courtesy Maritime and Seafood Museum.

Left: Within the antebellum Magnolia Hotel, restored and maintained by the City, are the colorful exhibits of the Mardi Gras Museum which trace the history of that event in Biloxi. Courtesy Mardi Gras Museum.

Right: Housed in the historic Point Cadet Coast Guard Station barracks, the Maritime and Seafood Industry Museum which opened in 1986 interprets the history of maritime Biloxi and its historic seafood industry. Courtesy Maritime and Seafood Industry Museum.

Below: The Biloxi Maritime and Seafood Industry Museum is the only maritime museum to own a pair of replicated historic sailing schooners. Modeled after the famed Biloxi oyster schooner, they serve as symbols of the city's proud seafood heritage. Seen here, the City logo emblazoned on their sails, are the *Glenn. L. Swetman* launched in 1989 and the *Mike Sekul* launched in 1992. Courtesy Maritime and Seafood Industry Museum.

Toward a New Millennium

In the early 1980s almost 25 percent of Biloxi's citizenry derived at least part of its income from tourism-related businesses. On the national scene, other historic, coastal communities like Biloxi were taking advantage of the public's ever-increasing leisure time. Waterside festival marketplaces were developed, and heritage tourism was emphasized. Hoping to strengthen its 150-year-old industry, city leaders pursued similar goals. The new Coliseum and Convention Center in west Biloxi was more vigorously marketed. In 1984 a Marine Education Center and Aquarium opened on the eastern tip of the peninsula in the midst of the historic Point Cadet factory district. A master plan was subsequently developed which called for revamping the entire Biloxi waterfront, including Back Bay estuaries, and highlighting the city's history, heritage, and culture. The effort included an historic preservation ordinance, patterned after those in other historic cities, and historic district guidelines for protecting the ambient character of individual neighborhoods. During the developmental process, more than five hundred historically significant residential, commercial, and institutional buildings were identified in the city. In 1986 a Seafood Industry Museum opened with interpretive exhibits featuring the city's rich, three hundred-year history. The construction of two replicated Biloxi oyster schooners in honor of the industry which for so many years had sustained Biloxi was undertaken by the museum.

A primary focus of the Waterfront Master Plan was the sand beach, a longtime tourist attraction. Since its creation in the 1950s, the sand beach had already undergone replenishment. A new bold plan called for the addition of pedestrian walkways, comfort stations, fishing piers, and landscaping. Commercial development and expanded marina facilities in selected areas were also recommended to increase waterfront utilization. Located on the eastern tip of the peninsula in the historic area once occupied by thriving seafood businesses, a major festival marketplace and marina was to be the crown jewel of the waterfront development project, mirroring successful ventures in several other historic Southern waterfront cities. (Landry et al. 1985)

Between August and November 1985 four hurricanes—Danny, Elena, Juan, and Kate—exasperated Biloxi's populace. Although three brought only heavy rains, a fourth, Elena, paid an unwelcome visit. After first threatening to strike the Mississippi Gulf Coast, the storm moved east to menace the central Florida coastline. Without making landfall, Hurricane Elena circled and returned, striking the Mississippi Gulf Coast on Labor Day, September 2, 1985. Having evacuated low-lying areas only days earlier, many coastians were just returning home. Elena's 110 mph winds arrived from the east, moving down the length of the coast and driving waters away from the Biloxi shore. Although escaping water damage, Biloxi experienced numerous tornadoes which felled trees and power lines throughout the city. So great was the volume of debris from trees in the Biloxi area that city leaders feared a major fire. The combined efforts of city workers, Keesler personnel, and volunteer groups were required for a rapid cleanup. (Sullivan 1989)

Wind damage from Hurricane Elena across the Mississippi Gulf Coast caused an insured loss of more than $352 million. In Biloxi numerous city departments and several local businesses and tourist attractions were temporarily displaced. However, city leaders did not retreat from their program of waterfront improvements. Although a festival market complex failed to develop, in 1987 the 280-slip Point Cadet Marina opened. At this same time Harrison County and municipalities all along the Mississippi Gulf Coast adopted a Sand Beach Master Plan which would guide waterfront development for years to come. Moreover, efforts to pump new life into the Vieux Marche' continued on schedule. When the new 147-bed Biloxi Regional Medical Center opened that same year, efforts were initiated to revive the historic downtown area as a professional office corridor.

As Biloxi moved into the last decade of the twentieth century, a surprising commercial turnaround began to unfold. In the 1980s after years of declining shrimp harvests and uncertain oyster landings, Biloxi seafood interests had shifted its focus to processing. In 1992 Biloxi captured a major share of the $400 million local seafood industry with its processing of more than fifty million pounds of domestic and imported shrimp. By the mid-1990s Biloxi seafood processors were employing almost three thousand full-time workers. At the same time oyster landings experienced a dramatic revival, reaching a twelve-year high. The seafood industry was once again recognized as a Mississippi Gulf Coast leader. Accompanying the revitalization of the seafood industry came the restoration of ancillary marine industries. (Biloxi Market Analysis 1997; MacKenzie et al. 1997)

Top: This view east toward the mouth of Biloxi Bay shows the modern Point Cadet Marina which opened in 1987. Lower right is its harbor master facility. Photo by author.

Bottom: A symbol of the change which has swept the Biloxi seafood industry since the 1980s are these massive steel-hull trawlers moored at a Back Bay processor with their booms pointed skyward. Courtesy Maritime and Seafood Industry Museum.

Taken from the same vantage points used by photographers almost a century ago, these images underscore the dramatic changes which have taken place in Biloxi. The views include above, looking west down Howard Avenue from the Lameuse Street intersection; middle, looking east along the waterfront atop the Biloxi lighthouse; and below, looking east toward Point Cadet from the small craft harbor near the location of the historic yacht club. Photos by the author.

Toward a New Millennium

6 Toward a New Millennium

Top: On February 14, 1699, Iberville first crossed the mouth of Biloxi Bay in a birch bark canoe while attempting to make contact with local Native Americans. Three hundred years later thousands of motor vehicles cross the same expanse daily. This view looks northeast from atop the Isle of Capri Casino. Photo by author.

Bottom: Almost a hundred years ago a photographer captured a streetcar passing near the two oaks in the center of this image. Although a pier still stands on the location of the once bustling ice wharf, little else remains of that era. Photo by author.

In this view looking south toward the intersection of Reynoir Street and Howard Avenue, the Saenger Theater, historic entertainment gem of another age, is dwarfed by the rising Beau Rivage Casino. Photo by author.

With a growing federal deficit, coast leaders feared the impact on the local economy of possible cutbacks in the government sector. With the seafood industry in a state of flux, the tourism industry appeared to be the only answer to Biloxi's uncertain future. In 1992 a county-wide casino gaming referendum approved dockside gaming for Harrison County. Biloxi stood perched on the brink of the greatest economic boom in its three hundred-year history! Within six months of the referendum three casinos were operating along the city's beachfront. Within two years eight were in operation and three others were under construction! Once the center of a bustling seafood industry, Point Cadet rapidly became the site of the largest concentration of dockside gaming institutions in the state. By 1997 Biloxi's casinos were generating approximately 35 percent of Mississippi's $2.2 billion gross gaming revenues! Because of a state requirement that dockside gaming institutions develop permanent land-based facilities, the growth of hostelries paralleled that of casinos. Moreover, the addition of hundreds of hotel rooms assured the city's development into a major convention city. (Biloxi Market Analysis 1997)

During the late 1990s, dockside gaming proved itself a catalyst for the growth of the tourism industry as well as a variety of casino support services in Biloxi. Major advertising efforts by the Harrison County Tourism Commission and local chambers of commerce led to significant increases in hotel occupancy, convention attendance, and attraction visitation. Between 1993 and 1996 the number of visitors grew from 1.5 million to more than 3 million annually, and tourism sales accounted for almost half of all retail sales in Biloxi. Not only did tourist numbers soar, but also employment, as the casino industry hired thousands of employees. As Biloxi headed toward its 1999 tercentenary, local casinos boasted fifty-five hundred casino resort hotel rooms and structures taller than any in the state under development. Thousands of additional employees for the developing hostelries presented Biloxi with problems it had not faced since the developing days of its historic oyster industry a century earlier. National awareness of Biloxi's many amenities, historic, environmental, and economic, attracted newcomers, including retirees, to settle in or near the resort community. The influx of population stimulated a demand for housing not seen since the arrival of Keesler more than a half century earlier. (*Sun Herald*, Oct. 29, 1997)

When the cold war ended in the mid-1990s, Keesler, headquarters for the Second Air Force and home of the Eighty-First Training Wing, witnessed a period of growth akin to Biloxi's. In addition to its mission as the electronics, computer, and weather training center of the United States Air Force, the base received additional personnel and programs as the Department of Defense instituted a cost-cutting base closure program. The base's vital role as one of the largest technical training centers in the Air Force secured its immediate future. By the late 1990s its desirable location, local amenities, and combination of health and other services had attracted almost ten thousand military retirees to the Mississippi Gulf Coast as well! Coupled with the number of uniformed base personnel and their dependents, the armed forces presence continued to be a major segment of the local population.

Taken in 1988, these two images show, above, the Central Beach area, and, below, Point Cadet, before the advent of casino gaming. Courtesy Tommy Triplett and Buford Myrick.

6 Toward a New Millennium

As Biloxi began planning for the celebration of its 1999 tercentenary, it concurrently developed a blueprint for its growth through the first two decades of the twenty-first century. Known by the sobriquet "Vision 2020," the comprehensive plan set goals and objectives for residential, commercial, and industrial development; parks, open space, and recreation; street and road improvements; public schools; and community facilities. Armed with tax revenues from gaming and almost universal commercial growth, the city began a myriad of road, drainage, parks, and facilities improvements even before the plan was adopted. As Biloxi enters the new millennium, and its fourth century, it does so with more optimism and brighter promise than at no other time in its past. With continued increases projected in per capita seafood consumption and a healthy national economy prompting increased leisure time, the future of both its historic seafood and tourism industries appears assured. In 1999 the city will have cause to celebrate more than just the arrival of the French some three hundred years ago, but its position as one of the most sparkling municipalities in the United States.

In this modern aerial image of Keesler Air Force Base, looking northeast, its "triangle area" of student dormitories and classrooms appears in the foreground. Parked adjacent to the runway in the distance are the weather reconnaissance aircraft of the 403d Wing (AFRES). Courtesy Keesler AFB.

The dramatic changes made to historic Point Cadet by dockside gaming are evident in this April 1998 image. Courtesy Miller C. Henry.

6
Toward a New Millennium

Taken during the May 1997 Blessing of the Fleet, this image shows the dockside gaming complexes which have emerged along the waterfront. Under construction in the foreground is the Beau Rivage Casino. Courtesy Miller C. Henry.

6

Toward a New Millennium

Bibliography

Abernethy, Thomas P. 1961. *The South in the New Nation, 1789–1819.* Baton Rouge: L. S. U. Press.

Allain, Mathe. 1988. *"Not Worth a Straw," French Colonial Policy and the Early Years of Louisiana.* Lafayette, Louisiana: Univ. of Southwest Louisiana, Center for Louisiana Studies.

Biloxi *Herald/Daily Herald/Sun Herald* (1884–1998).

Biloxi *Daily Herald Fiftieth Anniversary Souvenir Golden Jubilee Number,* Oct. 1934.

Brant, Irving. 1953. *James Madison, Secretary of State, 1800–1809.* Indianapolis: Bobbs-Merrill.

Brasseaux, Carl A. 1981. *A Comparative View of French Louisiana, 1699 and 1762: The Journals of Pierre LeMoyne Sieur d'Iberville and Jean-Jacques-Blaise d'Abbadie.* Lafayette, Louisiana: Center for Louisiana Studies.

Bureau of the Census. Census for: 1840, 1850, 1860, 1870.

Cain, Cyril R. 1953. *Four Centuries on the Pascagoula,* 2 vols. Spartanburg, South Carolina.

Camille Collection. Biloxi Maritime and Seafood Industry Museum.

Carstensen, Vernon. 1976. "Patterns on the American Land." *Surveying and Mapping* 36: 303–309.

Carter, Clarence E., ed. 1936–52. *Territorial Papers of the United States.* Washington.

Case, James E. 1971. "The Events Surrounding the Establishment of the Biloxi Air Corps Technical School." Unpublished MA Thesis: Univ. of Southern Mississippi.

Cassibry, Nap L. 1986. *Early Settlers and Land Grants at Biloxi,* 2 vols. Biloxi.

Chalmers, Charles O. 1937. "Report of the Executive Secretary of the Seashore Methodist Assembly, 1932–1937." Mississippi Department of Archives and History.

Chambers, Henry E. 1898. *West Florida and its Relation to the Historical Cartography of the United States.* Baltimore.

City of Biloxi Minute Books: 1886–1950

City of Biloxi Tax Map, 1940.

City of Biloxi Official Survey, 1930.

City of Biloxi Comprehensive Plan, 1979.

City of Biloxi Market Analyses: 1984, 1994.

City of Biloxi. 1996. Preliminary Draft of *Vision 2020: The Biloxi Comprehensive Plan.* Biloxi.

Claiborne, J. F. H. 1980 Reprint *Mississippi as a Province, Territory, and State with Biographical Notices of Eminent Citizens.* Baton Rouge: L. S. U. Press.

Clark, Thomas D. and John D. Guice. 1989. *Frontier in Conflict: The Old Southwest, 1795–1830.* Albuquerque: Univ. of New Mexico.

Conrad, Glenn R., trans. and ed. *Immigration and War, Louisiana: 1718–1721, from the Memoirs of Charles le Gac, former Director of the Company of the Indies in Louisiana.* Lafayette, Louisiana: Univ. of Southwest Louisiana.

Cox, Isaac J. 1918. *The West Florida Controversy, 1798–1810: A Study in American Diplomacy* Gloucester, Maine.

Cotterill Robert S. 1930. "The National Land System in the South, 1803–1812." *Mississippi Valley Historical Review* 126: 495–506.

Coulter, E. Merton. 1947. *The South During Reconstruction, 1865–1877.* Baton Rouge: L. S. U. Press.

Cummins, Light T. 1993. "An Enduring Community: Anglo-American Settlers at Colonial Natchez and in the Felicianas, 1774–1810." *Journal of Mississippi History* 55 (May) 133–36.

Dufour, Charles L. 1960. *The Night the War Was Lost.* New York: Doubleday.

Durrenberger, E. Paul. 1994. "A History of Shrimpers' Unions in Mississippi, 1915–1955." *Labor's Heritage* 5 (Winter) 66–72.

Dyer, Charles L. 1896. *Along the Gulf: An Entertaining Story of an Outing Among the Beautiful Resorts on the Mississippi Sound from New Orleans, La. to Mobile, Ala.* New Orleans.

Ezell, John S. 1975. *The South Since 1865.* Norman, Oklahoma: Univ. of Oklahoma Press.

Gallalee, Jack C. 1965. "Andrew Ellicott and the Ellicott Stone." *The Alabama Review* (April) 92–105.

Garraty, John A. 1968. *The New Commonwealth, 1877–1890.* New York: Harper & Row.

Garrett, Wilbur E., ed. 1988. *Historical Atlas of the United States.* Washington.

Giraud, Marcel. 1974. *A History of French Louisiana: The Reign of Louis XIV, 1698–1715.* Trans. by Joseph C. Lambert. Baton Rouge: L. S. U. Press.

Harrison County, Mississippi, Deed Books: 3, 9, 12, 15, 51, 66, 128, 141, 150, 183, 152. Gulfport, Mississippi.

Harrison County, Mississippi. *1925 Supervisors Map.*

Haynes, Robert V. 1952. "The Disposal of Lands in the Mississippi Territory," *Journal of Mississippi History* 24.

Holt, Hazel. 1968. "History of Biloxi," in *75th Anniversary of the First National Bank of Biloxi, 1893–1968.* Biloxi.

Howell, Grady H. 1991. *To Live and Die in Dixie: A History of the Third Mississippi Volunteer Infantry, C. S. A.* Jackson, Mississippi.

Husley, F. Val. 1993. "The Biloxi Schooner: Workhorse of the Northern Gulf," in *European Origins of the Small Watercraft of the United States and Canada.* Proceedings of the Museum Small Craft Association. Thibodeaux, Louisiana.

Hutchins, Thomas. 1968 reprint. *An Historical Narrative and Topographical Description of Louisiana and West Florida.* Gainesville: Univ. of Florida Press.

Irby Bobby N. and Della McCaughn. 1975. *Guide to the Marine Resources of Mississippi.* Hattiesburg, Miss.: Fox Printing Co.

James, Marquis. 1933. *Andrew Jackson: The Border Captain.* New York.

Jones, Ruth I. 1956. "Antebellum Watering Places on the Mississippi Gulf Coast." *Journal of Mississippi History* 18 (October) 268–92.

Journal of B. L. C. Wailes, August 23–27, 1852. Typescript in Mississippi Department of Archives and History. Jackson, Mississippi.

Kniffen, Fred B., Hiram F. Gregory, and George A. Stokes. 1987. *The Historic Indian Tribes of Louisiana: From 1542 to Present.* Baton Rouge: L. S. U. Press.

Landry, Bob et al. 1984. *Biloxi Waterfront: Facts and Opportunities.* Biloxi.

_____. 1985. *Biloxi Waterfront: Master Plan.* Biloxi.

Lang, John H. 1932. *A History of Harrison County.* Gulfport.

Lowery, Charles P. 1968. "The Great Migration to the Mississippi Territory, 1798–1819." *Journal of Mississippi History* (August) 173–92.

McKenzie, George C. 1967. "Report on Application of the City of Biloxi, Mississippi for Transfer for Historic Monument Purposes of Approximately 0.643 Acres of Surplus Federal Property—Biloxi Lighthouse, Biloxi, Mississippi." Washington.

MacKenzie, Clyde L. Jr. 1996. " History of Oystering in the United States and Canada, Featuring the Eight Greatest Oyster Estuaries." *Marine Fisheries Review* 58 (no. 4) 1–82.

MacKenzie, Clyde L. Jr. et al., eds. "The History, Present Condition, and Future of the Molluscan Fisheries of North and Central America and Europe: Vol. I, Atlantic and Gulf Coasts. *NOAA Technical Report NMFS 127.* Seattle.

McWilliams, Richebourg G., ed. and trans. 1981. *Iberville's Gulf Journals.* Tuscaloosa: Univ. of Alabama Press.

Maduell, Charles R. 1972. *The Census Tables for the French Colony of Louisiana from 1699 through 1732.* Baltimore: Genealogical Publishing Company.

Mahon, John K. 1972. *The War of 1812.* Gainesville: Univ. of Florida Press.

Malone, Dumas. 1970. *Jefferson the President: First Term, 1801–1805.* Boston: Little, Brown, Company.

Miller, Rudolph R. 1980. *Saga of the U. S. S. Biloxi, Biloxi Diary, and No Land for the Sailor: Two Graphic Accounts of the Exploits of the U. S. S. Biloxi (CL-80) 1943–1945.* New York.

Moore, Frank, ed. 1861–68. *Rebellion Record: A Diary of American Events,* 12 vols. New York.

Myer-Arendt, Klaus J. 1995. *Beach and Nearshore Sediment Budget of Harrison County, Mississippi: A Historical Analysis.* Jackson: Mississippi Office of Geology.

New Orleans *Daily Picayune* (1838–96).

Neuman, Charles J. and Brian R. Jarvin. 1987. *Tropical Cyclones of the North Atlantic Ocean.* Ashville, North Carolina.

Osborn, Kenneth W., Bruce W. Meghan, and Shelley B. Drummond. 1963. *Gulf of Mexico Shrimp Atlas.* Washington: Dept. of Commerce.

Owsley, Frank L. 1945. "The Pattern of Migration and Settlement on the Southern Frontier." *Journal of Southern History* 11 (May) 147–76.

Parrish, Patricia E. and Linda C. McFarland. 1991. *Keesler Air Force Base Then and Now, For Half a Century, a Leader in Technical Training, 1941-1991.* Keesler Air Force Base, Mississippi.

Pearcy, Arthur. 1991. *U. S. Coast Guard Aircraft Since 1916.* Annapolis.

Philbrick, Francis H. 1965. *The Rise of the West, 1754–1830.* New York: Harper, Row.

Pintado Papers. Historic New Orleans Collection. New Orleans, La.

Prucha, Francis P. 1969. *The Sword of the Republic: The United States Army on the Frontier, 1783–1846.* New York: MacMillan Company.

Rea, Robert R. 1990. *Major Robert Farmar of Mobile.* Tuscaloosa: Univ. of Alabama Press.

Rowland, Dunbar. 1978 reprint. *History of Mississippi, Heart of the South.* 4 vols. Spartanburg, South Carolina.

Rowland, Dunbar, ed. 1917. *Official Letter Books of W. C. C. Claiborne, 1801–1816.* Jackson, Mississippi.

Rowland, Dunbar and A. G. Sanders, eds. and trans. 1919–1932. *Mississippi Provincial Archives: French Dominion.* 3 vols. Jackson, Mississippi.

Schmidt, Aimee. 1995. "Down Around Biloxi: Culture and Identity in the Biloxi Seafood Industry." *Mississippi Folklife* 28 (Winter/Spring) 6–15.

Scholtes, Coleen C. and L. J. Scholtes. 1986. *Biloxi and the Mississippi Gulf Coast: A Pictorial History.* Norfolk: Donning Company.

Sheffield, David and Darnell Nicovich. 1979. *When Biloxi was Seafood Capital of the World.* Biloxi.

Sullivan, Charles L. and Murella Powell. 1985. *The Mississippi Gulf Coast: Portrait of a People.* California: Winsor Publications.

Sullivan, Charles L. 1989. *Hurricanes of the Mississippi Gulf Coast, 1713–Present.* Gulfport.

Swanton, John R. 1911. *Indian Tribes of the Lower Mississippi Valley and Adjacent Coasts of the Gulf of Mexico.* Washington: Smithsonian Institution, Bureau of American Ethnology.

The War of the Rebellion: A Compilation of the Official Records of the Union and Confederate Armies, 128 vols. Washington: 1880–1901.

The War of the Rebellion: A Compilation of the Official Records of the Union and Confederate Navies, 30 vols. Washington: 1894–1922.

Titler, Dale M. and Gary M. Murphy. 1981. *Keesler Field: Inception to Pearl Harbor, 1939–1941.* Keesler Air Force Base, Mississippi.

Toops, Connie. 1980. "The Biloxi Schooner," *Wooden Boat Magazine* 37 (Nov./Dec.) 81–84.

United States Coast Survey. 1851. *Survey Map of the Harbor and Back Bay of Biloxi.* National Archives: RG 23.

Vance, Ann. 1975. *An Historical Analysis of Colonial Land Grants in Mississippi.* Oxford, Mississippi: Coastal Management Program of the Univ. of Mississippi

Walthall, John A. 1980. *Prehistoric Indians of the Southeast: Archaeology of Alabama and the Middle South.* Tuscaloosa: Univ. of Alabama Press.

Walters, Vernon L. 1969. "Migration into Mississippi, 1798–1837." Unpublished thesis. Mississippi State University.

Weber, David J. 1992. *The Spanish Frontier in North America.* New Haven: Yale University Press.

Woodward, Comer V. 1951. *Origins of the New South, 1877–1913.* Baton Rouge: L. S. U. Press.

Index

A
Air Corps Station No. 8, 137
Apperson, J. W. Colonel, 120
Artesian Ice Company, 44
Avalez Hotel, 118, 119
Aviation Mechanics School, 137
Avondale Subdivision, 123

B
Baker, Ralph, 143
Bank of Biloxi, 55
Barataria Canning Company, 60
Barge Bottling Company, 149
Baricev's Restaurant, 142
Barq Building, 149
Bay of Pigs invasion, 150
Bay Terrace, 123
Beauvoir, 33, 70, 153
Berlin Wall, 150
Bienville Subdivision, 123
Bienville, 14, 19
Biloxi Airport, 130, 131, 132
Biloxi Bacon, 37
Biloxi Bay Addition, 123
Biloxi Bayou, 12
Biloxi Canning Company, 60
Biloxi Chamber of Commerce, 127, 132
Biloxi Community House, 145
Biloxi Country Club, 116
Biloxi Electric Railway, 63
Biloxi Golf Club, 103, 112, 124, 130, 137
Biloxi High School, 74, 122
Biloxi Light Plant, 55
Biloxi lugger, 145
Biloxi Machine Works, 127
Biloxi Maritime and Seafood Industry Museum, 159
Biloxi Regional Hospital, 150
Biloxi Regional Medical Center, 160
Biloxi Rifle Guards, 35
Biloxi Rifles, 36
Biloxi Roller Rink, 152
Biloxi Stadium, 130, 137
Biloxi Street Railway, 55
Biloxi tribe, 12, 14
Biloxi Yacht Club, 85, 152, 140
Biloxi-Ocean Springs Bridge, 126, 129, 154
Blessing of the Fleet, 167
Bohemians, 48, 78
Bowers, Eaton Jackson, Representative, 70
Brander, 135
Braun, Louis, Mayor, 132
Brielmaier and Foretich house, 158
Brierfield Subdivision, 123
Broadwater Beach Hotel, 123
Broadwater Hotel, 151
Broadwater Marina, 144
Buck Theater, 150
Buena Vista Hotel, 118, 120, 142, 153
Bungalow, 140
Bungelow Restaurant and Motel, 153
Burklin, E. G., 55
Byrenheidt, Andreas, Dr., 31, 32

C
Camp B. F. McClellan, 127
Carceaux, Nicholas, 21
Carquotte, John, 25
Carver, Elihu, 26
Cavelier de la Salle, René-Robert, 14
Chinn and Company flour mill, 57
Christian, Baptiste, 21
CL-80 USS *Biloxi*, 132
Claiborne, W. C. C., 24
Coast Automobile Club, 81
Coliseum and Convention Center, 160
Compagnies franches de la marine, 16, 19
Congressional Reconstruction, 38
Coral Gardens, 123
County of Charlotte, 20
Covacevich, "Fatty" Jack, 126, 135
Covacevich, "Jackie" Jack, 134
Crozat, Antoine, 16
Cuban Missile Crisis, 150

D
d'Iberville, Pierre Le Moyne Sieur, 12
Davis, Jefferson, 55
de Galvez, Don Bernardo, 20
de la Tour, Leblond, 17
de Merveilleux, M., 19
Depression, 135
Du Pratz, La Page, 19
Dukate Theater, 57
Dukate, William K. M., 44
Durocher, Andre, 25

E
Edgewater Gulf Hotel, 118, 156
Edgewater Hotel, 123
Edgewater Mall, 148, 156
Edgewater Subdivision, 123
Edmonds, S. P., Captain, 121
Elder and Bradford lumber yard, 57
Elks Club, 81
Ellicott, Andrew, 26
Elmer, F. William, 44
Emerald Beach Motel, 144

F
Farmar, Robert, Major, 20
Fayard, Angelique, 25
Fayard, Louis, 25
Felicity Methodist Church, 40
Fewell, James, Mayor, 36
Fiesta Motel, 153
Flood, William, Dr., 24
Fort Maurepas, 16
Fort Stoddard, 22, 27
Foster, William, 40
Fourth Military District, 38
French Minister of the Navy and the Colonies, 15
Friendship House, 140

G
Galle, Jules, 135
Gauld, George, 20

Gemmill's Bar-B-Q King, 144
Glenn L. Swetman, 159
Gorenflo and Company, William, 60
Gorenflo, William F., 44, 143
Great Migration, 28
Guice, Julia, 148
Guice, Wade, 148, 152

H
Handsboro, 29
Harbor Light Restaurant, 152
Harrison County Development Commission, 143
Harrison County Seaway, 143
Harrison County Tourism Commission, 163
Harrison, Pat, Senator, 131, 138
Harrison, William Henry, President, 29
Hearts Ease Park, 70
Holmes, David, Governor, 27
Hotel Riviera, 85
Howard Primary School No. 2, H. T., 122
Howard, John D., 35
Hurricane Betsy, 148
Hurricane Camille, 150, 152, 154
Hurricane Elena, 160
Hurricane Ethel, 148
Hurricane Flossy, 148
Hurricane Frederic, 158

I
Iberville, 14, 16
Isle of Caprice, 120

J
Jackson, Andrew, General, 27
Jackson, Andrew, President, 70
Jefferson, Thomas, 22
Johnson, Lyndon, President, 150
Joullian and Company, E. C., 60
Joyner Subdivision, 123

K

Keegan's Bayou, 122
Keesler Air Force Base, 164
Keesler Field, 102, 138
Keesler, Samuel Reeves, Jr., Lieutenant, 138
Keller Golf Links, 63
Keller, J. H., 40
Kendall Brick works, 32
Kennedy Hotel, 60, 132
Kennedy, John, Mayor, 124
King George II, 22
Klein's Bakery, 150
Kuljis oil dock, 134

L

Ladner, Claude, 25
LaFontaine, Pierre, 25
Lamar Beach, 123
Law, John, 16
Lopez and Dukate Cannery, 60
Lopez, Lazaro, 44, 60
Louis XIV, 16
Louisiana Purchase, 21, 22, 23
Louisville & Nashville depot, 129
Louisville & Nashville railroad, 60
Lyons, Matt, 149

M

Madison, James, 22, 24
Magnolia Hotel, 159
Mardi Gras Museum, 159
Marine Conservation Commission, 148
Marine Education Center, 160
Maritime and Seafood Industry Museum, 125, 159
Mary Margaret, 134
Mathurin, Jacques, 25
Mathurin, James, 21
Matthes, Carl, 124
Maurepas, 15
Maycock, John, 44
McLaurin, A. J., Governor, 55
Methodist Camp Ground, 124
Mike Sekul, 159
Military Assistance Program, 150
Miramar Addition, 123
Miramar Park, 127
Mississippi City, 29
Mississippi Coast Coliseum and Convention Center, 155
Mississippi Coast Shipbuilding Company, 98
Mississippi Coast Traction Company, 70
Mississippi Power Company, 70
Mississippi Territory, 22

Missonet, Pierre, 25
Monroe, James, 22
Montross Hotel, 85
Moore factory, G. B., 141
Moran, Fred, 135

N

Naval Reserve Park, 124, 127, 130, 136, 137
Naval Reserve Subdivision, 123
Naval Reserve Tract, 135
Naval Reserve, 70, 102
New Orleans Mobile Mail Line Company, 35
New Orleans, Mobile, and Chattanooga Railroad, 38
Nouveau Biloxi, 17
Nouveau Orleans, 17

O

Oak Park Subdivision, 125
Oak Park, 123
Ohr, George, 57
Old Brick House, 158
Old Spanish Trail Highway, 127
Old Spanish Trail National Highway, 118
Ord, E. O. C., General, 38

P

Pakenham, Edward, General, 27
Parker, U. A., 135
Pass Christian-Point Cadet Road, 29, 41
Pass Road, 29, 32, 37, 156
Pastime Cafe, 152
Pattison Pontiac Showroom, 152
Peoples Bank, 55
Pettus, John J., Governor, 36
Peytavin, Antoine, 21, 25
Pine Hurst Addition, 123
Poindexter, George, 27
Point Cadet Marina, 160, 161
Point Cadet, 140, 142, 154, 160, 162, 163, 164
Popps Ferry Bridge, 124, 132
Popps Ferry, 122, 125
Province of West Florida, 20

Q

Question Mark Lounge, 150

R

Ragusin, Anthony, 130, 132, 136
Reynolds, Mary, 36
Rhodes Point, 143
Richards, Dosette, 25
Roosevelt, Franklin, 129
Roosevelt, Theodore, President, 70

Rosell Sash and Blind Factory, 57
Ryan, Abram, Father, 40

S
Saenger theater, 156
Sand Beach Master Plan, 160
Saucier, Philippe, 25
Scholtes, Joe, 134
Seafood Capital of the World, 46
Seafood Industry Museum, 160
Seligmann, John, 57
Shipyards, 126
St. Denis, Juchereau de, 12
Stengel, Casey, 124
Sun'n Sand Motel, 153
Swanzy, John, 131

T
Territory of Orleans, 24, 27
Third Mississippi Infantry, 37
Thirty-First "Dixie" Division, 131
Tivoli Hotel, 118
Treaty of Paris, 1783, 22
Treaty of San IldeFonso, 21
Treaty of San Lorenzo, 21
Triple XXX Cafe, 141

U
Unger Subdivision, 123
United States Coast Survey, 32

V
Vardaman, James K., Governor, 64
Vieux Marche, 156, 160

W
Wailes, Benjamin, 32
West Biloxi Strip, 144, 156
West Florida Revolt, 23, 28
White House Hotel, 81, 103
White-winged queens, 46, 81
Wilkinson, James, General, 27
Wood, Leonard, General, 102

Y
Yeager, Benny, 135

About the Author

A native Biloxian whose ancestors immigrated from Switzerland in the 1850s. Val Husley received his doctorate in history from Mississippi State University in 1970. After military duty in Vietnam he taught history and served as an academic administrator at West Virginia Institute of Technology. He returned to Biloxi in 1984 as the City's historical administrator and helped develop the Maritime and Seafood Industry Museum and other city historical assets.

As curator of the Maritime and Seafood Industry Museum, Val has labored for more than a decade to bring national awareness of the history and heritage of Biloxi and its life-giving historic seafood industry.

Author of numerous articles on the American Civil War, American South, and maritime history, Val also has designed, constructed, and illustrated a wide range of museum exhibits nationally. As a member of a variety of historical organizations, his interests have also led him into living history reenacting and competitive shooting with historical firearms. His hobbies include crafting Pennsylvania Rifles and other historically accurate eighteenth- and nineteenth-century firearms.